THE NORMAN CONQUEST
OF ENGLAND

JANICE HAMILTON

TWENTY-FIRST CENTURY BOOKS
MINNEAPOLIS

This book is dedicated to all those who enjoy a good story.

Consultant: David M. Perry, Assistant Professor of History, Dominican University, Chicago, Illinois

Primary source material in this text is printed over an antique-paper texture.

The image on the cover is of the French fighting in the Battle of Hastings. It is a detail from the Bayeux Tapestry, which is wool embroidery on linen and was created before the year 1082. It is at the Musée de la Tapisserie, Bayeux, France.

Twenty-First Century Books
A division of Lerner Publishing Group, Inc.
241 First Avenue North
Minneapolis, Minnesota 55401 U.S.A.

Website address: www.lernerbooks.com

Library of Congress Cataloging-in-Publication Data

Hamilton, Janice.
     The Norman conquest of England / by Janice Hamilton.
          p.   cm. — (Pivotal moments in history)
     Includes bibliographical references and index.
     ISBN 978–0–8225–5902–3 (lib. bdg. : alk. paper)
     1. Great Britain—History—Norman period, 1066–1154—Juvenile literature.
     2. William I, King of England, 1027 or 8–1087—Juvenile literature. 3. Normans—Great Britain—Juvenile literature. I. Title.
     DA195.H36 2008
     942.02'1—dc22   2006102629

Manufactured in the United States of America
1 2 3 4 5 6 – DP – 13 12 11 10 09 08

CONTENTS

CHAPTER ONE
ANGLO-SAXON ENGLAND

The law of the thane [landowner] is that he be entitled to his chartered estates, and that he perform three things in respect of his land: military service and the repair of fortresses and work on bridges. Also in many estates further land duties arise by order of the king, such as [looking after the] deer-fence at the king's residence, and equipping a guardship and guarding the coast, and attendance on his superior, and [supplying a] military guard, almsgiving and church dues.

—Rights and Ranks of People, c. A.D. 1050

1066: most British schoolchildren are as familiar with this year as U.S. students are with 1776. The year 1066 marked a turning point. That year, invaders from Normandy, in northern France, crossed the waters of the English Channel to England. Led by William, the duke of Normandy, the invaders conquered England at the Battle of Hastings. In the years after the battle, Norman rulers greatly changed English society.

This English coin from the eleventh century bears a portrait of William. Before the Battle of Hastings, he was William, duke of Normandy. After the Battle of Hastings, he was King William I of England, or William the Conqueror.

At the time of the Norman Conquest, the people of England felt angry and humiliated by the invasion. But modern-day British people, the descendants of the conquered English and the Norman conquerors, also have reason to be proud: 1066 proved to be the last time foreigners succeeded in invading their island nation.

Two groups—the English and the Normans—clashed at the Battle of Hastings. At the time of the battle, both sides had turbulent histories filled with intrigue and violence. Both England and Normandy had very close connections to Scandinavia (the northern European nations of Denmark, Norway, and Sweden). After the battle, a new society emerged in England.

Northern Europe
A.D. 1066

NORWAY

SWEDEN

SCOTLAND

NORTH
SEA

DENMARK

IRELAND

ENGLAND

WALES

London •

N

ATLANTIC
OCEAN

English Channel

NORMANDY

BRITTANY

FLANDERS

- - - Regional border
• City

Miles
0   50   100   150

0   100   200
Kilometers

It had closer ties to France and western Europe than to
Scandinavia. The English language changed, with new
words and literary traditions introduced from France.
Architecture changed too, as did social customs, government, and the economy.

"ENGLA-LAND"

England is located on Great Britain, an island off the northwestern coast of Europe. At the time of the Norman

Conquest, in 1066, people had inhabited Great Britain for thousands of years. The island was first home to Stone Age peoples. Around 600 B.C. a group called the Celts arrived from mainland Europe and moved throughout Great Britain. The Celts also lived on a neighboring island, Ireland.

In A.D. 43, the Romans invaded Great Britain. The Romans were based in Italy but had expanded their empire to include much of Europe. Calling the land Britannia, the Romans ruled southern Great Britain for almost four hundred years. They built roads across the island. They designed towns, including London, with streets arranged in tidy rectangular grids.

Romans built Hadrian's Wall in what is now northern England. Along the wall, forts like this one (only its foundation remains) kept out northern raiders in the second century.

In the 400s, the Roman Empire broke apart. Roman soldiers left England. Soon afterward, Germanic tribes settled in Great Britain. They were the Angles, Saxons, and Jutes, who together came to be known as the Anglo-Saxons. They took control of the south and east of Great Britain, while the Celts remained in the north and west, as well as in Ireland.

The name England emerged during this period. It came from the term *Engla-land*, meaning "Angle land." This was also the beginning of the medieval period, or Middle Ages. This period in European history lasted from the 400s through the 1400s.

The early Anglo-Saxon era was an unsettled period.

Warrior-kings controlled different parts of England and fought with each other constantly. The first king to control a large portion of England was Offa, who ruled from 757 to 796. Egbert was the first king to bring all the English people into one kingdom. In principle, the witenagemot, or witan, an assembly of wealthy and powerful men, selected a new king when an old one died. In reality, kings often took the crown by force.

This portrait of King Offa is from a fourteenth-century English text called the Golden Book of Saint Albans.

CONVERTING THE ENGLISH

In 596 Pope Gregory, the leader of the Christian Church in Rome, sent about thirty missionaries to England. Their leader was an Italian monk named Augustine. In 597 they succeeded in converting England's King Ethelbert to Christianity. By the end of the year, more than ten thousand Anglo-Saxons had followed suit.

Early Anglo-Saxons had been pagans. That is, they had believed in many gods and spirits. But missionaries (religious teachers) had converted them to Christianity around 600. The Christian Church became powerful in England. It owned great amounts of land. Church officials called bishops were wealthy and influential men. The church gave its blessing to each new king.

FARM LIFE AND TOWN LIFE

Most people in Anglo-Saxon England were farmers. They lived in close-knit communities, celebrated together during religious and other festivals, enjoyed traditional songs and folktales, and mourned together when death or disaster struck. Their survival depended on good weather and a successful harvest. When the crops failed, people sometimes died from hunger.

Most Anglo-Saxon farmers could not afford their own land. Instead, most rented small plots of land from landowners

This illustration comes from the Julius Work Calendar. Created around A.D. 1020, the calendar shows English people working throughout the months of the year. These men are harvesting grain in August.

called thanes. The thane's estate was called a manor. It was like a small village, with a church, a mill for grinding grain, workshops, pastures for livestock, ponds and streams for fishing, and forests for hunting and gathering wood. Each manor also had a huge, unfenced field where the villagers farmed. Teams of oxen pulled heavy plows through the soil, carving long, narrow furrows for planting crops.

In the most common arrangement on a manor, the farmers were serfs. Serfs were bound to the land where they lived, meaning they could not leave and live somewhere else. They remained on the land, even if a new thane bought it. The thane, who was the lord of the manor, gave each serf family a small piece of land to farm. In exchange for this land, serfs worked the thane's land as well. They performed other tasks for the thane, such as cutting wood and building fences. Male serfs had to serve military duty when the thane needed to raise an army. In addition, serfs had to pay taxes to their thanes, usually in the form of crops from their own land.

Other farmers on the manor were free peasants. Unlike serfs, they were not bound to the land. They were free to come and go. They rented land from the thane, paying rent in the form of crops, money, labor, or military service. Still other farmers on the manor were slaves. Slaves were like property. They could be bought or sold apart from the land. In exchange for labor, thanes provided their slaves with basic necessities, such as food and shelter.

The typical manor contained about five hides of land (a hide varied from about 40 to 120 acres, or 16 to 48.6 hectares). At the center of the manor, the thane's family

ANGLO-SAXON SLAVERY

Slavery was widespread in Anglo-Saxon England, but only the wealthy owned slaves. People ended up as slaves in several ways. Some were foreigners captured in war. Others were English people put into slavery as punishment for their crimes. Hard times sometimes forced people to sell themselves or their children into slavery. Slaves lived much like everyone else in an Anglo-Saxon village. They lived in small homes with their families and usually worked as farmers. In exchange for their labor, lords provided basic necessities for their slaves. For example, a slave owner had to give a female slave "eight pounds of corn for food, one sheep or threepence for winter supplies . . . whey [a watery but nutritious part of milk] in summer or one penny."

lived in a fortified home called a manor house. In times of danger, such as an enemy invasion, everyone on the estate took shelter in the manor house. The thane protected the villagers in other ways too. For instance, he settled disputes and enforced the law.

A small number of English people (about 10 percent) lived in towns, where they worked as craftspeople and merchants. London was the largest English town. Towns often

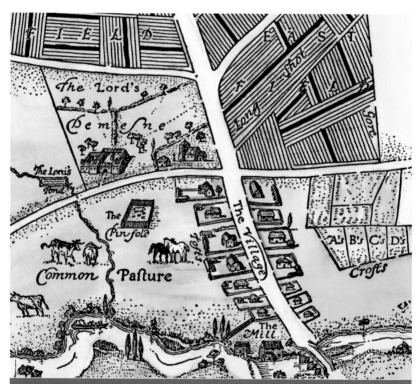

This woodcut shows a medieval estate in England. Agricultural fields, village buildings, pasture lands, the lord's home, and other areas are clearly marked. The mill, where villagers ground their grain, was set next to a river. Crofts, on the left side of the image, were rented fields.

had two roles: they served as fortresses, with high walls and other defenses, and they were trading centers. English merchants traded mainly with merchants from France, Germany, and Scandinavia. The English exported mostly woolen cloth. They imported pottery, wine, and stones for sharpening farm tools. Some traders imported luxury goods from distant lands, such as silk, gold, ivory, glass, and spices.

Music and entertainment were common in both villages and towns. Musicians playing horns, harps, and other instruments entertained both rich and poor. Jugglers, acrobats, and puppeteers put on shows. Chess, dice games, and ball games were popular pastimes.

This illustration from a thirteenth-century French songbook shows noblewomen playing a ball game in a garden.

ANGLO-SAXON RIDDLES

The Anglo-Saxons enjoyed creating and solving riddles. These poetic puzzles usually described everyday things. A number of them were recorded in the *Exeter Book*, a collection of old verses that the bishop of Exeter gave to his cathedral in 1072. Here are a few samples:

1. I'm told a certain object grows
   in the corner, rises and expands, throws up
   a crust. A proud wife carried off
   that boneless wonder, the daughter of a king
   covered that swollen thing with a cloth.

2. On the way a miracle: water becomes bone.

3. The wind wafts little creatures
   high over the hill-slopes. They are very
   swarthy, clad in coats of black.
   They travel here and there in hordes all together,
   singing loudly, liberal with their songs.
   Their haunts are wooded cliffs, yet they sometimes
   come to the houses of men. They name themselves.

(Answers: 1. bread 2. ice 3. house martin, a type of bird)

HOMES AND GARDENS

The typical Anglo-Saxon family lived in a one-room house. The dwelling had a fire pit at the center. The fire provided warmth and heat for cooking, although the smoke must have stung people's eyes. The roof, made of straw or reeds, had a hole above the fire pit to allow smoke to escape. Windows were not common in Anglo-Saxon homes, so houses were dark inside. If a home did have windows, they were generally covered with thin animal skins. Glass was too expensive.

Houses were made of wood. Some were coated with a layer of cob—a mixture of clay, straw or horsehair, and cow dung or sand. Cob was a strong, long-lasting building material that could be molded into different shapes. The ingredients were readily available, and cob kept houses cool in summer and warm in winter. But Anglo-Saxon homes were quite vulnerable to fires because the building materials burned easily.

A garden grew outside every house. Families cultivated apples, pears, cherries, onions, carrots, radishes, parsnips, parsley, and cabbage for their own meals. In the common field outside the village, people grew wheat, the staple of the Anglo-Saxon diet. Every August 1, Lammas Day (Bread Mass Day), villagers held a festival to celebrate the first loaf of bread made from the new harvest.

Loaves of bread were round and flat. The bread itself was coarse. People often dipped pieces of bread into thick vegetable soup to soften it. In addition to bread, Anglo-Saxons ate meat and fish. In the fall, men killed wild pigs that roamed the woods outside their villages. People usually fished with weirs, or funnel-shaped nets, which they set in rivers.

Villagers raised sheep for their wool. The spinning wheel had not yet been invented, so women spent many hours using hand spindles to make thread. Using looms, they wove the thread into cloth. They fashioned the cloth into simple tunics, leggings, and other garments, sometimes tinted with red, orange, and yellow dyes made from vegetables. The coarse, homespun fabric was probably itchy, especially in summer. Cotton was unknown in Anglo-Saxon England, and only the rich could afford linen garments.

RELIGIOUS LIVES

The Anglo-Saxons were devout Christians. They believed that God intervened in their everyday lives. Every village had a small church, made of wood or stone. All villagers attended church regularly and observed religious holidays. On Easter, Christmas, and other holy days, priests put on short plays to bring religious messages to their congregations. Some Anglo-Saxons went on pilgrimages, or trips to holy places. They went to Rome, headquarters for the Christian Church, and even to Jerusalem, a holy city in the Middle East.

The Anglo-Saxons revered saints—men and women who had led holy lives or made great sacrifices for their faith. People often prayed to saints for help with problems. Every Anglo-Saxon church kept relics—bones and other objects associated with saints—in its altar. People believed that relics carried saints' powers and therefore could cure illnesses and bring about other miracles. People would flock from miles around to see, touch, or be near them.

DEATH AND DISEASE

Diseases such as smallpox and cholera were widespread in Anglo-Saxon England. Drinking water was often contaminated with disease-causing organisms. Many children died before reaching adulthood, and most adults died before age fifty. Anglo-Saxon doctors knew nothing about germs and very little about disease. They thought that excess blood caused sickness, so they frequently used leeches (bloodsucking worms) to draw blood from patients. Doctors and other healers also treated illnesses with plants and herbs. While many of these remedies were effective, others may have done more harm than good.

This illustration comes from a fourteenth-century Italian medical book. It shows a man with bloodsucking leeches on his legs. Doctors often used leeches to treat disease in the Middle Ages.

BOOKS AND MANUSCRIPTS

Although most Anglo-Saxons could not read, the English produced many books in the eleventh century. They were carefully copied and often beautifully illustrated by monks. At this time, Latin was the language of learning and of the church in Europe. The Anglo-Saxons produced some texts in Latin, but they also created a rich variety of poetry, religious books, and other documents in their native language, Old English. Books of homilies (short religious sermons or lectures on right and wrong) were common. Some books were psalters, or collections of sacred poems. Other books recounted the lives of saints.

Illuminated manuscripts were documents illustrated with patterns, large decorative letters, and pictures of people and animals. Some manuscripts featured scenes in bright red, blue,

Even though they were Christians, the Anglo-Saxons retained some of their old pagan gods and superstitions. Many people believed that elves, fairies, and trolls inhabited the forests that surrounded their villages. They recited charms to ward off evil and disease.

Religious centers called monasteries flourished in Anglo-Saxon England. Monasteries were home to monks, men who devoted their lives to prayer and meditation. As well as religious communities, monasteries were centers of learning and green, and gold. Others had delicate outline drawings. Most portrayed scenes from the Bible. One document, called the *Julius Work Calendar*, showed ordinary peasants at work throughout the year. Other Europeans admired Anglo-Saxon illuminated manuscripts. Monks in other parts of Europe sometimes copied English styles.

This eleventh-century illustration of the Biblical story of Noah's ark is from an Old English version of the Bible.

the arts. They were also farms. Their grounds held dormitories and churches, libraries with beautiful handwritten manuscripts, agricultural fields, meadows for livestock, ponds for fish, and wooded areas.

CLASS DIVISIONS

Anglo-Saxon society was divided by class and rank. Slaves and serfs were at the lowest level of society. Free farmers and merchants ranked somewhat higher. Next came the thanes, earls, and high church officials. The king was at the peak of society. In the Anglo-Saxon world, people always referred to those of higher standing as "lord" or "lady."

Thanes and earls were part of the nobility—they were men with land, power, and privilege. Most thanes inherited their land and their position in society from their parents.

OLD ENGLISH

The people of Anglo-Saxon England spoke a language they called Englisc (English). Modern scholars call it Old English. It was based on the Germanic languages of the Angles, Saxons, and Jutes. Many legal documents, poems, and historical accounts, including an important book called *The Anglo-Saxon Chronicle*, were written in Old English.

Many modern English words have their origins in Old English. These words include *king* from *cyning*; *now* from *nu*; *answer* from *andswaru*; *island* from *igland*; *hear* from *hieran*; and *old* from *eald*.

The most common words for "woman" in Old English were *wif* and *wifman*. They have their modern equivalents in *wife* and *woman*. Both words are related to an Old English word meaning "weaving." Cloth making, including weaving, spinning, and embroidery, were among a woman's chief responsibilities in Anglo-Saxon England.

RIGHTS AND OBLIGATIONS

In the early eleventh century, the manager of a large estate wrote a document called *Rights and Ranks of People*. In it, the writer described the duties and the rights of everyone on an estate. Although he noted that customs differed from one estate to another, he set out the basic duties of thanes and serfs. He listed payments due to people who looked after the lord's pigs, oxen, and other animals, and to the beekeeper and the cheese maker. According to the document, a servant "ought to have what he might earn in twelve months from two acres, one sown and the other unsown; he is to sow the one himself; and he ought to have his food and shoes and gloves. If he can earn more, he is to keep the profit himself."

Thanes who accumulated considerable wealth and power were known as magnates. Some magnates worked directly for the king. Earls also controlled great wealth, land, and power. Each earl acted as the king's representative in a certain region, called an earldom. Sometimes the king appointed earls. Sometimes an earl's son succeeded him in the position. Earls often had great influence with the king and helped him run the government.

Among the upper classes, it was common for men to pledge homage, or loyalty, to a man of higher standing. When this happened, the man of lower standing was called the vassal; the man of higher standing was called the lord. Vassals pledged homage to lords at special ceremonies. Once

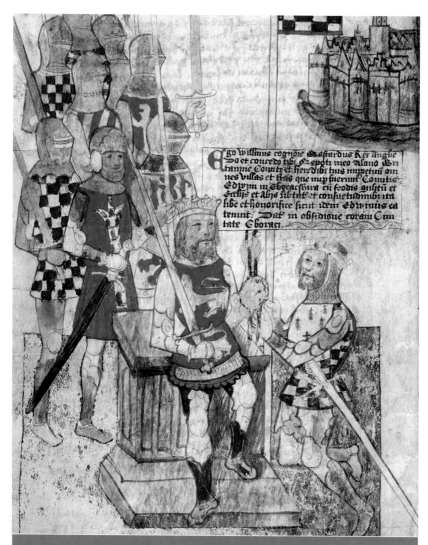

A knight pays homage to William the Conqueror in this fifteenth-century English manuscript illustration.

he had sworn his loyalty, a vassal had to serve his lord, usually by fighting in his army and paying him taxes. For his part in the bargain, the lord protected the vassal from enemies. Sometimes lords gave their vassals large parcels of land.

HOW MUCH ARE YOU WORTH?

In Anglo-Saxon England, a person's status was measured by his or her wergild, meaning "man price." If someone was killed, the killer had to pay wergild to the dead person's family. A male serf had a wergild of two hundred shillings, while a thane's wergild was twelve hundred shillings. A woman's wergild depended on whether she was a slave or free, a virgin, married, or widowed.

THE ANGLO-SAXON KING

In Anglo-Saxon times, England had no official capital. The king and his court constantly moved around the countryside. In this way, the king could meet personally with his subjects and allow different thanes to serve him. The witan worked with the king to issue laws, negotiate with foreign powers, impose taxes, and defend the country. Members of the witan also elected new kings.

Anglo-Saxon England had two types of laws: customary and written. Customary laws were unwritten rules of conduct. They differed from one area to another. Written laws applied throughout the kingdom. England had a well-organized system of local courts, which tried people for everything from petty theft to cattle rustling, sexual assault, murder, and treason. According to the laws of King Canute, passed between 1020 and 1023, "if anyone commits a deed punishable by outlawry, the king (alone) is to have power to grant him peace [pardon]."

WOMEN IN ANGLO-SAXON ENGLAND

By studying wills and other documents, historians have learned about the lives of women in Anglo-Saxon England, especially the lives of wealthy women. Unlike women in many places at the time, upper-class Englishwomen had the right to own land. Upon death, many noblemen left valuable property, including land, to their wives, sisters, and daughters. A woman could not

This early nineteenth-century British illustration shows an Anglo-Saxon noblewoman standing in front of a carriage.

be forced to live in a nunnery (a religious community for women) or forced to marry a man she disliked. Women often married young, sometimes as young as twelve, and wealthy parents usually arranged their daughters' marriages. When a couple married, they signed a contract that protected the woman's interests. The husband agreed to look after his wife properly and to give her a "morning gift," usually money or land. A married couple's wealth belonged to both husband and wife together. A woman with children was entitled to half her husband's possessions when he died. An Anglo-Saxon woman also had the right to leave her husband. A man found guilty of raping a woman had to pay a fine, although the fine varied according to the woman's social position.

We know less about the lives and rights of women of lower classes. Few people could read and write in Anglo-Saxon England. Ordinary women did not write diaries or letters that can give us insights into their lives. But historians do know that lower-class women usually worked as farm laborers. They tended crops and animals, milked cows, and made food and clothing for their families. Other women worked for the nobility, usually as nursemaids or household servants. In towns, some women earned money by washing clothes, selling bread, or weaving. Sometimes, if a male merchant died, his widow took over his business.

Anglo-Saxon England also had an efficient financial system, and this system made Anglo-Saxon kings very wealthy. Kings owned vast royal lands. They could seize the lands of citizens who committed serious crimes. They collected money from tolls (user fees on roads and bridges) and collected rent in the form of food in some regions. The greatest portion of a king's income came from taxing his citizens. The main tax, the geld, paid for the king's army, navy, and other projects. The king and the witan raised and lowered the geld as needed.

Anglo-Saxon kings maintained a small army of trained, professional foot soldiers called housecarls. Earls also had housecarls. In peacetime, housecarls spent little time with their lords. Many lived far away. But if war broke out, they were ready to serve immediately.

Anglo-Saxon England also had a militia, or citizen army, called the *fyrd*. By law, the inhabitants of each five hides of land had to send one soldier to serve in the fyrd for two months each year. In this way, England always had about fifty thousand men available for military service. It is not known how men were chosen for service. What is clear is that members of the fyrd had little training or experience in combat. Deserters were severely punished. The law said that "the man, who in his cowardice deserts his lord or his comrades, whether it is on an expedition by sea or one on land, is to forfeit all that he owns and his own life; and the lord is to succeed to [take over] his possessions and to the land which he previously gave him."

Church and state were closely linked in Anglo-Saxon England. Once a king was on the throne, people believed that he ruled by God's will. The coronation, the ceremony in which a new king was crowned, took place in church. A priest anointed the king with holy oil as a symbol of God's blessing. When they wrote laws and made decisions, the king and his advisers always adhered closely to church teachings.

CHAPTER TWO
THE KINGS OF ENGLAND

> Then [the commander of the Anglo-Saxon army] bade the
> warriors advance, bearing their shields, until they all stood
> on the river bank. Because of the water neither host [army]
> might come to the other. There came the tide, flowing in
> after the ebb; the currents met and joined. All too long it
> seemed before they might clash their spears together.
>
> —"The Battle of Maldon," Anglo-Saxon poem, c. 990s

By the late 700s, England was a prosperous and productive
nation. Its wealth began to attract the interest of Vikings,
pirates based in Scandinavia. Sailing fast ships, Viking raiders
periodically crossed the North Sea to England. They stole
coins and other valuables, killed innocent civilians, and took
prisoners. Viking raiders also destroyed Anglo-Saxon books,
legal papers, and other documents. With fewer books available, learning quickly declined in English monasteries.

THE VIKINGS

The Vikings came from modern-day Scandinavia. They were farmers as well as traders, explorers, and pirates. Between about 750 and 1060, Vikings traveled south to mainland Europe and east to Russia. They even sailed across the Atlantic Ocean to Iceland, Greenland, and North America. Some were looking for new land to farm. Others were raiders who attacked and robbed the local people. Vikings established settlements in many areas, including England, Ireland, and Normandy. In their new homes, Viking settlers retained some of their Scandinavian customs. But they also adopted the traditions of their neighbors, including Christianity.

To protect his people against Vikings, King Alfred, who ruled from 871 to 899, built a series of fortresses throughout southern England. Called *burhs*, these fortresses had high walls, with room for houses and shops inside. In case of an attack, people took their families and livestock to the nearest burh for protection. Burhs were strategically located so that no settlement was more than 20 miles (32 kilometers), or a day's march, from a burh.

English kings continued to build burhs into the early 900s. England also developed its civilian army, the fyrd, during this period. To pay for these defenses, kings devised a system of national taxation. Although the Vikings continued to attack, the burhs and fyrd kept Viking raiders from penetrating deep inside English territory.

THE LIFE OF KING ALFRED

Asser, a Welshman who taught Latin to young Alfred, wrote a biography of the ruler, *The Life of King Alfred*, in 893. Like other royal biographers, Asser made sure to paint Alfred in a positive light. The following story from the biography tells us that Alfred was a gifted boy who was eager to learn:

A nineteenth-century engraving of King Alfred

Now on a certain day [Alfred's] mother was showing him and his brothers a book of Saxon poetry, which she held in her hand and finally said, "Whichever of you can soonest learn this volume, to him will I give it." Stimulated by these words, or rather by divine inspiration, and allured by the beautifully illuminated letter at the beginning of the volume, Alfred spoke before all his brothers, who, though his seniors in age, were not so in grace, and answered his mother: "Will you really give that book to that one of us who can first understand and repeat it to you?" At this his mother smiled with satisfaction, and confirmed what she had said: "Yes," said she, "that I will." Upon this the boy took the book out of her hand, and went to his master and learned it by heart, whereupon he brought it back to his mother and recited it.

ETHELRED THE REDELESS

In 979 King Ethelred II came to the English throne. He was neither a strong ruler nor a good military leader. People called him Ethelred the Redeless, meaning "unwise" or "badly advised." Later, historians mistakenly changed the name to Ethelred the Unready.

In 991, during Ethelred's reign, Danish Vikings attacked England. "The Battle of Maldon," an Anglo-Saxon poem, describes the encounter. The poem tells how English forces reached the battle site while the Vikings were still camped on an island in the Blackwater River, northeast of London. The overconfident English commander allowed the enemy to cross to the mainland. He "bade the warriors advance, bearing their shields, until they all stood on the river bank." This decision

This silver penny shows Ethelred II. It was minted in Lewes, in southern England, in the early eleventh century.

cost him his life and led to an English defeat. After their loss
at Maldon, the English gave regular tribute, or payments, to
the Vikings. To raise the tribute money, the English government charged a tax on land. This tax was called the Danegeld.

For help in defending England, King Ethelred made an
alliance with the duke of Normandy. To cement the alliance,
Ethelred married Emma, the duke's daughter. Nevertheless,
Sweyn, a Danish prince, conquered and destroyed more
English territory. English nobles were so unhappy with
Ethelred that in 1013 they made Sweyn the king of England.
After Sweyn's death, the witan assembled to choose a new
king. They selected Sweyn's son Canute, on the condition
that he provide good government. In addition to ruling
England, Canute was also king of Denmark and Norway.

BEOWULF

The best known Anglo-Saxon
poem is *Beowulf (a page from
an eleventh-century Old
English version is pictured at
right)*. It is an epic, or
extremely long, poem, written
by an anonymous poet,
probably in the eighth century
A.D. It is the story of Beowulf,

Vikings raid the coast of England in this late nineteenth-century hand-colored woodcut.

a Swedish prince who helps the king of the Danes by killing two monsters. He returns home and is killed by another monster. At one point, the poem describes a fire-breathing dragon:

> Then the dragon began to breathe forth fire,
> to burn fine buildings; flame tongues flickered,
> terrifying men; the loathsome winged creature
> meant to leave the whole place lifeless.
> Everywhere the violence of the dragon, the venom
> of that hostile one, was clearly to be seen.

THE VENERABLE BEDE

In Anglo-Saxon England, monks were often writers and scholars. The printing press had not yet been invented, so monks copied books and other documents by hand. One of the most important scholars of the era was Bede, known as the Venerable (honorable) Bede. Bede was born about 672 in Northumbria. At age seven, he moved to a monastery to study with monks. He lived in the monastery for the rest of his life, devoting himself to the study of the Bible. Writing in Latin, Bede explained the meaning of Bible passages and recounted the lives of saints and church leaders. His *Ecclesiastical History of the English People*, completed in 731, is one of the few written sources describing the early Anglo-Saxons. Bede popularized a method of dating events from the time of Christ's birth, using the designation anno Domini (the year of our Lord), or A.D. This dating system became the accepted one, still used in modern times.

A page from Bede's Ecclesiastical History of the English People *from the eighth century.*

CANUTE THE GREAT

When Canute became king of England in 1016, he abandoned his wife. He married Emma, widow of Ethelred, who had died that year. Like many unions of the time, Canute's marriage to Emma was more about politics than love. This marriage sealed his alliance with the Normans. Emma sent her children by Ethelred—sons Edward and Alfred and daughter Godgifu—to live with her family in Normandy. Canute and Emma later had a son, Hardecanute.

King Canute, as shown in this eighteenth-century engraving, was king of England, Denmark, and Norway at the same time.

Canute reigned over England peacefully for twenty years. People respected him as a courageous warrior and an efficient administrator. He and his advisers passed a series of new laws. One law pledged that people "above all things . . . would ever love and honor one God and steadfastly hold one Christian faith, and love King Canute with due loyalty."

Canute made an important change in government: he divided southern England into four earldoms—Wessex, Mercia, East Anglia, and Northumbria—each governed by an earl. In Wessex, Canute gave the job of earl to Godwin, an ambitious and powerful man. As king of Denmark, Norway, and England, Canute had to travel for long periods. The earls ran the English government while he was away.

CANUTE'S SUCCESSORS

Canute died in 1035. He had said that Hardecanute, his son with Emma, should succeed him. But by then, Hardecanute was already governing Denmark and had little time for England. Thus the witan decided that Harold Harefoot, son of Canute and his first wife, would rule England temporarily.

Around this time, Ethelred's son Alfred returned from Normandy with a group of friends—perhaps to visit his mother, Emma. As the son of a former king, he presented a threat to the current king. Godwin, acting on behalf of Harold Harefoot, arrested Alfred and had some of his friends killed. An unidentified assailant then attacked Alfred, and he died from his wounds. The witan, believing Godwin to be responsible for the attack, tried him for his role in Alfred's death but did not find him guilty.

In 1040 Harold Harefoot died, and Hardecanute became king. His reign was brief and unimpressive. He died in 1042. At that point, the witan chose Edward—Emma's only living son—to rule England.

EDWARD THE CONFESSOR

Edward, known as Edward the Confessor because of his great religious faith, was thirty-eight and unmarried when he

This thirteenth-century English manuscript illustration shows Edward (center) at a banquet.

came to the throne. Previous kings had relied on their military abilities to keep control of the country. But King Edward lacked military skill and was not a strong leader. He was very religious and was more interested in building a great church (Westminster Abbey in London) than in running the country. He also had a fiery temper. He regularly exiled (banished) his enemies from England, only to later forgive them and allow them to return.

Having spent the previous twenty-five years outside England, King Edward knew little about the country he ruled. He spoke more French than English. So during the early years of Edward's reign, a group of nobles, including Godwin, acted as the power behind the throne.

To increase his family's power, Godwin arranged for King Edward to marry his daughter, Edith. Edward suspected Godwin's involvement in the death of his brother, Alfred. But he needed Godwin's political support and may even have been afraid of the earl. As for the arranged marriage, Edward may have felt that marrying an Englishwoman would prove to the nation that he was truly English. Edward also appointed several of Godwin's sons as earls.

Godwin, like many other English people, resented Edward's Norman friends and influences. Furthermore, the two men had very different personalities. The king was serious and selfish. Godwin was outgoing and assertive. They grew to dislike each other intensely.

The rivalry between Godwin and the king's Norman friends came to a head in 1049. A French count was returning home after visiting King Edward. He and his armed followers stopped in

This tablet is Godwin's seal, used to mark official documents. Godwin would have pressed the tablet into hot wax affixed to a document. The engraved text says, "the seal of Godwyn the thegn [thane]."

Dover, a town in Wessex, and demanded lodgings for the night. When the head of one household refused to let them in, fighting broke out. Some twenty people were killed and many more injured. The count returned to the king and complained about his treatment in Dover. Without investigating the circumstances, Edward ordered Godwin to attack Dover to punish its residents. Godwin refused.

Knowing that refusing to follow the king's orders was a serious offense, Godwin prepared his followers for battle with the king. Edward also ordered his army to get ready for combat. The country was on the brink of civil war. However, neither side really wanted a fight. They realized that war between England's leaders would only weaken the country and leave it open to attack by foreigners. As a compromise, the two sides agreed to trade hostages (prisoners taken in previous conflicts).

Nevertheless, King Edward forced Godwin and his family to leave England. They went into exile in Ireland and in

EXILE

From the earliest civilizations to modern times, governments have used exile, or forced absence from one's homeland, to punish people or to control political opponents. Governments often exile their enemies to prevent them from rallying their supporters. (Imprisoning or killing opponents as an alternative might make them even greater heroes to their followers.) Exile was a common form of punishment in Anglo-Saxon times.

Flanders (around present-day Belgium). Edward's dislike of the Godwin family had by then grown so strong that he even banished his own wife, Godwin's daughter Edith, to a nunnery. With Godwin and his family gone, Edward appointed some Norman friends to important positions in government. He also began thinking about who would succeed him as king, since he had no children.

THE SEEDS OF CONFLICT

Sometime in late 1051 or early 1052, William, the duke of Normandy, paid an official visit to England. Edward and William held private conversations. No one knows exactly what they said, but many historians believe that Edward told William he wanted the duke to succeed him as king of England. Not only were the men distant relatives through the Norman-born Queen Emma, but William's father had protected the young Edward during his years in Normandy. If William became king, the alliance between England and Normandy would strengthen, helping to close the English Channel to enemies. For William, the appeal of the English throne was obvious. A king in eleventh-century England had a great deal of power. He owned vast expanses of royal land. His country was wealthy, and it traded with other nations far and wide. Not only William but other leaders in northern Europe had designs on the English throne.

The political map of England soon changed when the exiled Godwin and his sons returned to England. Before the end of 1052, they had organized a fleet of supporters who were eager for a fight. The witan intervened. It held a

This illustration from an Old English illustrated Hexateuch (the first six books of the Bible) shows an English king and his witan (an assembly of wealthy and powerful men). The king holds a scepter and a sword.

meeting at which Godwin defended his decision to refuse the king's orders. Godwin's testimony won over the witan. Again, England's leaders had avoided civil war.

But King Edward had lost the battle of wills. His Norman advisers realized that the people of England resented them. They left for Normandy. Humiliated, Edward had to allow the Godwin family to take back their estates and their influence. His wife, Edith, also returned to his side.

Godwin died in 1053, and his son Harold Godwinson became the king's closest adviser. His title was earl of Wessex, but he effectively ruled the whole country. King Edward was less and less interested in politics, and Harold proved to be both a loyal subject and an efficient leader.

The remaining years of King Edward's reign were generally peaceful, with one exception. Tostig, one of Harold Godwinson's brothers, ruled the northern earldom of Northumbria. In 1065 people there rebelled. They accused Tostig of overtaxing them and having his Northumbrian enemies murdered. To put down the rebellion, King Edward and Harold Godwinson allowed a new earl to take control in Northumbria. They forced Tostig to leave England.

CHRISTMAS 1065

By 1065 King Edward's health was failing. In December of that year, the witan gathered at a royal palace near London

In this illustration, an artist imagines the scene at Edward's deathbed. The image shows the archbishop of Canterbury standing at the foot of the bed, Harold Godwinson kneeling, and a servant tending to the dying king. Also at the foot of the bed, Edith weeps for Edward.

for its regular Christmas meeting. Many church leaders were also in town to attend the opening of Westminster Abbey, the church that Edward had spent years planning. When the church opened on December 28, Edward was too sick to attend the ceremony.

On January 4, 1066, the king woke from a troubled sleep and spoke to the people gathered around him. They included his wife, Edith, who was warming his feet in her lap, Harold Godwinson, and the archbishop of Canterbury. Edward told them of a dream in which devils came to England, bringing fire, swords, and war. He addressed his wife, saying that she had always served him with devotion. Then, according to *The Life of King Edward*, the king stretched out his hand to Harold and said, "I commend [entrust] this woman and all the kingdom to your protection." He died later that day or the next and was buried in Westminster Abbey on the morning of January 6.

CHAPTER THREE

NORMANDY

He [William] thus deprived of a father in the years of his youth, was brought up by the shrewd foresight of his guardians in such a way as to develop his naturally noble attributes. During his minority [youth] many of the Normans, renouncing their fealty to him, raised earthworks in many places and constructed for themselves the strongest castles. When they felt themselves thus sufficiently secure, a number of them immediately rebelled, stirred up sedition, and inflicted cruel destruction upon the country.

—*William of Jumièges*, The Deeds of the Norman Dukes, c. 1070

Normandy lies in modern-day France, just across the English Channel from England. Like Great Britain, France was once part of the Roman Empire. Vikings began attacking northern France in the early 800s. They burned the city of Rouen and advanced inland as far as Paris.

Exiled from his native Norway, a Viking named Rolf arrived in France in the late 800s. He established a base at the mouth of the Seine River. Rolf and his followers slowly

Vikings under the command of Rolf invade France via the Seine River in this late nineteenth-century hand-colored woodcut.

expanded the area they controlled. In 911, unable to remove the Vikings from the region or stop their destructive raids, the king of France made an agreement with Rolf. He granted the Vikings control of the lower Seine valley in exchange for peace and military assistance. As part of the arrangement, the pagan Rolf became a Christian and swore loyalty to the king.

NORMANDY AND FRANCE

When the Romans invaded Great Britain, they also controlled Gaul (modern-day France). At the time, Gaul was home to Celtic peoples. By the late 400s, Roman power had declined. Several Germanic tribes, including the Franks, invaded Gaul. By the early 500s, the Franks outnumbered the Celts in Gaul. The region was eventually named France, after the Franks.

The greatest king of the Franks was Charlemagne, who ruled from 768 to 814. A tireless warrior, he expanded his kingdom into a vast Christian empire. He established courts of law, introduced new coins, and gathered leading scholars at his court. Art and architecture—especially the construction of churches and monasteries—flourished during his reign. Charlemagne brought a stable government to France. He divided the nation into administrative units, with a duke or count in charge of each. He granted large estates to trusted nobles. In return, they were responsible for maintaining roads, bridges, and fortifications on their land.

Charlemagne's descendants ruled France until 987. But the kings of France became progressively weaker. Nobles became more powerful, and some dukes ruled their own regions almost as independent nations. The best-organized and most powerful such region was Normandy.

Normandy took its name from Rolf and the other Viking "north men."

Although they maintained some of their Scandinavian customs, the Vikings in Normandy became absorbed into French culture. They became French speakers and abandoned their pagan practices for Christianity. They also adopted the French system of government, devised by King Charlemagne (Charles the Great) in the 800s. Under the French system, the Norman ruler was called a duke.

The unique mixture of French and Scandinavian traditions distinguished Normandy from its neighbors. Furthermore, the many merchants and other travelers who passed through Normandy on their way to the English Channel introduced the Normans to ideas from other parts of Europe. Theoretically, Normandy was part of France. But it acted as an independent state.

Some Normans worked as fishers or shipbuilders. Others were farmers. Aided by a mild climate and fertile soil, Norman farmers grew wheat, barley, and grapes. They raised cows and horses. Most people lived in small villages, where they followed customary laws and farmed common fields. The largest towns in Normandy included Rouen, Bayeux, and Caen.

Like the wealthy Anglo-Saxons, upper-class Normans were linked in a network of lords and vassals. Some vassals were knights, soldiers who fought on horseback. Knights worked for wealthy landowners called barons. In exchange for land, knights fought for barons on the battlefield and guarded their castles.

NORMAN KNIGHTS

When a boy from a noble Norman family was about seven or eight years old, he had to choose his future career. He had only two options: he could become a man of the church, or he could become a chevalier—"a man of the horse." If he chose the church, he would become not only a religious leader but also a scholar. He would learn to read and write and perhaps teach.

If he became a chevalier, or knight, he began training in his lord's house. A young trainee was called a page. He learned to ride, hunt, and fight, but not much else. At age sixteen, he became a squire. He put on armor and learned to handle a long spear called a lance. In his twenties, he became a full knight.

Many young Norman men were trained in the art of war. But in the absence of a threat from a foreign enemy, they had little to do. This situation caused problems. Many knights were available for hire. Barons amassed small, private armies of knights and fought among themselves. It was the peasants and other

WILLIAM OF NORMANDY

William, the future duke of Normandy, was born around 1028 in the town of Falaise. His parents, not married to one another, were Duke Robert I and a young woman named Herleve. Historians know little about her, but they think that her father was a tanner (a craftsperson who makes

This fourteenth-century French manuscript illustration shows pages helping the knights they serve prepare for battle.

citizens who suffered most, as warring knights destroyed crops and burned buildings throughout the countryside.

animal hides into leather). Later, Herleve married a nobleman and had two other sons, Odo and Robert.

Duke Robert had become the leader of Normandy when his older brother, who preceded him as duke, died suddenly. Robert and his brother had long been bitter rivals, and some people accused the new duke of murdering his brother.

Fighting between their supporters split the region. In 1031 Robert's uncle, the archbishop of Rouen, worked out a truce between Robert and his enemies. This truce brought some peace to Normandy.

In 1034 Robert decided to go on a pilgrimage to Jerusalem. Like the Anglo-Saxons, the Normans had strong Christian beliefs, and pilgrimages were common. Wealthy people often set off on pilgrimages with many followers and servants. The large group was meant to impress those they passed on the road. But pilgrimages could be risky undertakings. Accidents, bandits, and disease claimed the lives of many pilgrims. So before he left, Robert wanted to make sure his young son, William, would succeed him as duke if he did not return.

OTHER NORMAN CONQUESTS

England was not the only place the adventurous Normans found themselves. In the early eleventh century, Normans on pilgrimages to Jerusalem passed through southern Italy. There they helped Italian leaders fight pirates and dictators. Soon many Norman mercenaries (soldiers for hire) made their way to Italy, where their skills in warfare made them rich. They fought for whoever paid the best. Around the middle of the eleventh century, Normans gained a foothold in southern Italy, where they owned great castles and estates.

Robert persuaded Normandy's barons to recognize William as his heir. He also presented the boy to King Henry I of France. In a ceremony, William paid homage to Henry and became the king's vassal. In turn, the king was obligated to protect the boy. Sure enough, Robert fell ill and died on the pilgrimage in 1035. William, age seven, succeeded his father as duke.

William was not only still a child, he was also the child of unwed parents, which made some people look down on him. These weaknesses made him vulnerable to those who did not want him to be duke. William lived with his mother's family. On

This eighteenth-century engraving shows King Henry I of France. At first, Henry protected Duke William from his enemies. But later Henry and William became enemies themselves.

several occasions, Herleve's brother had to sneak William out of the house in the night to hide him from enemies.

With shaky leadership, Normandy became a violent society. Long-standing feuds and rivalries between barons flared up. Barons prepared their private armies to go to war with each other, inflicting "cruel destruction upon the country." William's enemies had most of the young duke's supporters stabbed, poisoned, or thrown into dungeons.

Worried about the unrest in Normandy, and bound to assist his young vassal, King Henry helped William. Henry essentially governed Normandy as his own territory until William became an adult. By 1047, no longer a child, William was governing Normandy on his own. Some nobles supported him. They served as his tax collectors and judges and defended his territory with their strategically placed castles.

In 1047 an ambitious noble from western Normandy tried to overthrow William. He wanted William's title—and all the wealth and power that came with it. He and his followers plotted to kill William while the young man was visiting the west, but William learned of the plan and escaped on horseback during the night. The story of how he rode across the dark countryside and forded rivers at low tide became a local legend.

King Henry brought his army to Normandy and helped William take on the rebels in the Battle of Val-ès-Dunes. William of Poitiers, a knight who fought at the battle and later became William's biographer, said that William "was undismayed by the sight of [his enemies'] swords. Hurling himself upon them, he terrified them with slaughter." However, William could not have won the long and bitter battle without the help of King Henry's troops.

The events at Val-ès-Dunes proved to be only a warm-up to William's struggles. For another seven years, he was constantly at war with enemies in Normandy and elsewhere. It was during this period, in about 1051, that William went to England and met with King Edward. Perhaps that was when William first came to believe that he could not only be duke of Normandy but also king of England.

Meanwhile, King Henry turned against William, perhaps hoping to gain control over Normandy for himself. The king allied himself with the powerful count of Anjou and other nobles. The king's forces attacked William's army at Mortemer in 1054. No details of this battle survive, but the outcome was clear: William pulled off a stunning victory and proved himself to be a strong military leader. The victory at Mortemer solidified his authority over Normandy.

This seventeenth-century statue of Matilda of Flanders, William's wife, stands in the garden of the Palais du Luxembourg, Paris.

William's personal life was no less turbulent than his political life. He married Matilda, the daughter of the count of Flanders and the niece of King Henry. The marriage caused much controversy. At first the pope, the head of the Christian Church, forbade the couple to marry. Historians continue to debate what his objection was. Some think the pope objected because William and Matilda were too closely related, since both were descended from Rolf the Viking. They married anyway, and eventually a new pope approved the union. In gratitude the couple built two magnificent abbeys, or monasteries, in the town of Caen.

This is one of the two abbeys at Caen, France, built by Matilda and William in the mid-eleventh century.

William's life quieted down. In 1060 his two greatest enemies, King Henry and the count of Anjou, died. At this point William was in his early thirties. He was tall, strong, and courageous. Like many trained warriors in Norman society, he was a brutal man. He could be ruthless in killing his enemies. He had also proved himself as a military commander. He had the support of many noble families and the backing of the church. These factors combined to make William's Normandy one of the most powerful regions of Europe.

WILLIAM'S CLAIM TO THE CROWN

William believed he would someday become king of England. Two events led to this belief. First was the meeting with King Edward around 1051, when the two rulers may have discussed the succession. The second event took place in 1064, although different accounts of the event contradict each other.

According to Norman sources, England's Harold Godwinson traveled to France that summer. No one knows the reason for his trip. Norman sources say that King Edward sent Harold with a message for William, confirming that William was in line to be the next king of England. Other sources disagree. They suggest that Harold merely set off on a hunting or fishing trip and was blown across the English Channel by a storm.

Whatever his intentions, Harold landed not in Normandy but in a neighboring territory, Ponthieu. There the local count imprisoned him. When William heard what had happened, he demanded Harold's release, and the count let Harold go. William entertained Harold at his palace in Rouen. Then Harold accompanied his host on a raid against neighboring Brittany. During the raid, William impressed Harold with his fighting skills. Harold made an oath of fealty (loyalty) to William, and William made Harold a Norman knight.

According to Norman sources, Harold also promised to help William secure the throne after Edward's death. Not only was this a promise, it was a sacred, unbreakable oath, made on the relics of a saint. The Bayeux Tapestry—an embroidery that tells the story of the Norman Conquest in pictures—shows Harold standing next to large reliquaries

The Bayeux Tapestry tells the story of the Norman Conquest from the Norman point of view. This section of the tapestry shows Harold (right) swearing fealty (loyalty) to William. The two boxes beside him are reliquaries (containers for relics).

THE BAYEUX TAPESTRY

The Bayeux Tapestry is one of the most important records of the events of 1066. It is a series of pictures embroidered in wool on a piece of linen. It measures more than 230 feet (70 m) long and 20 inches (50.8 centimeters) wide. The illustrations, accompanied by Latin descriptions, portray the events of the Norman Conquest, from Harold's trip to Normandy to his death at the Battle of Hastings. The tapestry focuses on Harold swearing an oath to help William become king and then breaking that promise. Historians think that Odo, William's half-brother and the bishop of Bayeux, ordered the tapestry to be sewn at an abbey in Canterbury, England. It may have been completed by 1077. The tapestry is on display at a museum in Bayeux, France.

(containers for relics) during this event. But another source, written many years later, says that William tricked Harold by hiding the relics until after he had made the promise.

Again, no one knows whether or why Harold took this oath. Some historians suggest that Harold did so under pressure. After all, he couldn't leave Normandy without William's permission and help. Or perhaps the prospect of William as king, and himself as a chief adviser, was appealing to Harold. Whatever the details of these events, it is clear that William expected to become the king of England upon Edward's death.

CHAPTER FOUR

A QUESTION OF SUCCESSION

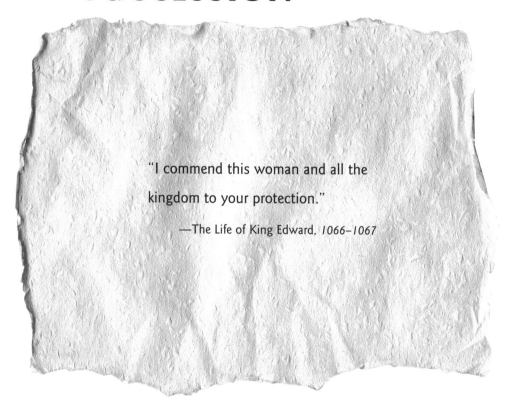

"I commend this woman and all the
kingdom to your protection."

—The Life of King Edward, 1066–1067

With King Edward's death, it was up to the witan to
make the final choice about who would succeed him as king
of England. According to traditional guidelines, the new
monarch needed the character to rule with strength and justice. He had to be an *aetheling*, which meant "thronewor-
thy." In other words, he had to be a member of the royal
family. And he had to be English.

The witan quickly elected Harold Godwinson as King

This section of the Bayeux Tapestry illustrates Edward's death in 1066.

Harold II. He had been with Edward at his deathbed. In his dying words, Edward had entrusted his wife and his kingdom to Harold, although no one knows for sure whether Edward meant that Harold should succeed him as king.

Some members of the witan had reservations about Harold, who did not meet all the qualifications for the throne. Although he was English, he was not of royal blood. His family had pursued power ruthlessly in the past. But the witan probably realized that the kingdom needed a strong leader, and Harold had demonstrated his leadership abilities. Then in his early forties, Harold was good-natured, patient, tolerant, and kind, but he could be tough when necessary.

Harold II's coronation took place in Westminster Abbey on the afternoon of January 6, 1066. The archbishop anointed him with holy oil. Those present prayed that he would defend the church and the English people. He received symbols of power, including a ring of unity, a crown of glory and justice, and a sword of protection, but he hardly had time to celebrate.

WESTMINSTER ABBEY

In the 1040s, King Edward decided to rebuild a small monastery near his palace on the banks of the Thames River. That monastery was originally founded around 960. Edward enlarged it and built a large stone church in honor of Saint Peter. The church was first known as the west minster (a minster is a kind of church), to distinguish it from Saint Paul's Cathedral, which was the "east minster." Later its name became Westminster Abbey. Edward died just as the church was completed, and he was buried in front of the altar. Almost a year later, William was crowned there. In the 1200s, King Henry III rebuilt the abbey in the Gothic style of architecture.

Westminster Abbey has been the setting for the coronations of almost every English monarch since 1066. It has also hosted royal funerals, weddings, and other special occasions. Many kings and queens are buried there, as are poets, scientists, and warriors.

Harold is crowned king of England in Westminster Abbey in this section of the Bayeux Tapestry.

WILLIAM WANTS THE CROWN

When William of Normandy learned that Harold had been crowned king of England, he was furious. He was disappointed and also humiliated, since he had bragged about taking the English throne. He immediately sent a message of protest to Harold. No one knows what William said. But whatever it was, efforts to find a compromise failed. The English and the French began to prepare for war.

William told his barons that he planned to seize the English crown. Many were skeptical, especially since William had no witnesses or documents to prove his claim to the throne. But William used several arguments to justify an invasion, including revenge for the murder of King Edward's brother, Alfred, many years before. Although Godwin (King Harold's father) had been cleared of Alfred's murder, many people still suspected he had had something to do with it. William also argued that Harold had committed a sin when he went back on his oath sworn on sacred relics.

THE GODWIN FAMILY

The Godwin family was the most powerful family of eleventh-century England. The first famous Godwin emerged from unknown origins to become a close adviser to King Canute. Canute appointed him earl of Wessex, a huge earldom that stretched across southern England. Godwin later became a powerful figure in the court of King Edward.

Godwin married into the Danish royal family and had several children: Svein was exiled for criminal behavior. Harold followed in his father's footsteps as a royal adviser and earl. He eventually became king. Tostig was earl of Northumbria until the people there rebelled against him. He later attacked England with the king of Norway and died at the Battle of Stamford Bridge. Gyrth and Leofwine, both earls, died at the Battle of Hastings. Wulfnoth lived much of his life as a hostage in Normandy. Godwin's daughter, Edith, married King Edward.

The Norman barons did not want to anger William. They also had good reason to join him. England was a wealthy nation. If the Normans achieved success, great wealth would be their reward. Over the course of the next few months, the duke persuaded each baron to provide a certain number of knights and foot soldiers and to build boats to transport them to England. Many mercenary soldiers, seeking the profits of war, joined William's force.

To attract broader support for the project, William appealed to the church. He sent representatives to the pope in Rome. They argued that the English church needed reform. The church in England had developed in partial isolation from European influences. It was not well organized. Many English priests were married, a forbidden practice in most other places. The Normans said that the English church needed to be brought under tighter control by Rome.

The English did not send representatives to the hearing because they probably didn't know about it. So with only the Norman argument to consider, the pope, Alexander II, agreed to support the Norman mission. He gave the Normans a papal banner to carry into battle.

Pope Alexander II agreed to support William's invasion of England. With the backing of the church, the Normans believed their cause was a righteous one.

William wore sacred relics around his neck. These symbols not only inspired William's troops to have courage but also inspired them to fight in the name of their faith.

With the pope's blessing, knights and foot soldiers from Normandy, Flanders, Brittany, and other regions flocked to the cause. They knew they stood to benefit with land or wealth if William won. All summer the shipwrights and

This detail of the Bayeux Tapestry shows men transporting arms and armor to load onto ships bound for England.

carpenters of Normandy built a fleet to carry the army and its horses across the English Channel.

William's plan to invade England was daring. He made no secret of his plans, so his troops would not be able to surprise the English. Instead, they had to make a quick, aggressive attack. The job would be difficult. It was hard to transport men and horses across rough seas in open boats. In addition, Norman vessels of the time could not sail into the wind. They could sail only with the wind directly behind them. The Normans required a wind from the south to carry them to England. The fleet was ready by mid-August. But the wind blew from the north for a month, preventing the Norman crossing.

In early summer, King Harold had ordered watchmen to guard cliffs and harbors all along the coast where the Normans were expected to arrive. He sent a large portion of the fyrd to the Isle of Wight, an island off England's south coast. There at least ten thousand armed men, mostly thanes, settled in for the summer to wait for the invasion. The English navy was also ready. It consisted of several hundred open boats, with high curved ends and single square sails. The boats were designed to carry soldiers but not to fight at sea. They, too, waited on the beaches of the Isle of Wight.

Finally, on September 8, the English forces gave up waiting. With winter coming on, Harold must have decided there would be no attack until the spring of 1067. After all, crossing the channel in winter in small boats was unsafe. England had never been invaded in winter before. Harold ordered the fyrd to go home. He instructed the navy to proceed up the Thames River to London.

THE ANGLO-SAXON CHRONICLE

One of the main sources of information about early English history is a group of documents called *The Anglo-Saxon Chronicle (a page is shown below)*. The documents contain yearly descriptions of wars, the deeds of kings, and other historical events. The first part of the chronicle, created in 891, records events from the 400s up to 891. Monks compiled this information from earlier documents. After 892, various writers added brief reports of each year's events. The final entry was made in 1154. These documents provide much of what we know about the reigns of King Alfred and King Ethelred, as well as the Norman Conquest.

SURPRISE ATTACK

In mid-September England was attacked—but not by the Normans. Harold Hardraade, the king of Norway, landed his forces near the city of York in northeastern England. As king of Norway, he had a weak claim to the English throne, based on an alleged agreement between his predecessor in Norway and Hardecanute, the king of Denmark. Like William, Harold Hardraade intended to take the English throne by force.

His fleet of approximately three hundred ships had benefited from the north wind that was keeping William's ships in port. His troops sailed down the coast of Scotland and

Viking ships under the control of Harold Hardraade land on the coast of England in this nineteenth-century hand-colored woodcut. Harold Hardraade's invasion took the English by surprise. The main English army was far to the south. Only a small English force was nearby to face the invaders.

rowed up the Humber River toward York. By his side was Tostig, King Harold's brother and the former earl of Northumbria. Tostig had spent the last few months in exile, first in Flanders and then in Scotland. Tostig pledged to help the Norwegian's cause, probably believing that he would regain his earldom in return.

News of the Norwegians' arrival reached King Harold in London on September 19. Harold immediately started to lead about two thousand mounted housecarls north. Before he could arrive, however, the Norwegians met other English troops at the Battle of Fulford. The English troops, and the two earls who commanded them, were inexperienced in battle. The invaders were hardened warriors. The fighting was over quickly, and the city of York surrendered to Harold Hardraade and Tostig.

The invaders demanded some five hundred English hostages. Then they waited by their ships, resting and feasting for several days. The hostages were to be delivered to a place called Stamford Bridge on September 25. On the appointed day, Harold Hardraade left about one-third of his soldiers with the ships. The others accompanied him to Stamford Bridge, about 13 miles (21 km) away. The Norwegians did not expect to encounter any resistance. Although they brought their helmets and weapons, most left their protective armor behind.

When Harold Hardraade and his soldiers reached the bridge, they were amazed to find King Harold and his army waiting. Harold had marched day and night to cover 190 miles (305.7 km) in just a few days. Along the way many citizens had joined up with the fyrd.

When the opposing forces came face to face, Harold talked with his brother Tostig. They did not reconcile. Then the two armies confronted each other across a small river. They fought in hand-to-hand combat with battleaxes, swords, and spears. One account says that a huge Norwegian warrior stood on a bridge and defended it single-handedly, killing any Englishman who tried to cross. Eventually an English soldier found a boat, floated under the bridge unnoticed, and speared the Norwegian through a gap in the boards.

The Battle of Stamford Bridge lasted all day. Although a great many English soldiers were killed, King Harold proved his skill as a commander. Both Harold Hardraade and Tostig were killed. So many invaders died that the survivors need-ed only twenty-five ships for the return trip to Norway.

King Harold (right) looks away from the bodies of his brother Tostig (left) and the Norwegian king, Harold Hardraade (lying center), after the Battle of Stamford Bridge in 1066. This image is part of a nineteenth-century British engraving.

CHAPTER FIVE
THE BATTLE OF HASTINGS

Then Count William came from Normandy to Pevensey on Michaelmas Eve [September 28] and as soon as they were able to move on they built a castle at Hastings. King Harold was informed of this and he assembled a large army and came against him at the hoary [frosted] apple-tree. And William came against him by surprise before his army was drawn up in battle array. But the king nevertheless fought hard against him with the men who were willing to support him, and there were heavy casualties on both sides.

—The Anglo-Saxon Chronicle, *1100s*

One day after the Battle of Stamford Bridge, on the night of September 26, the wind changed direction along the coast of France. William immediately ordered his soldiers to board the waiting boats with their horses. The Normans crossed the channel on the night of September 27.

William's ship, the *Mora*, sailed in the lead, with a lantern hanging from its mast. When the sun came up in the morning, William and his crew saw neither land nor the rest of the fleet. The crew members were close to panic, but William sat down and enjoyed a leisurely breakfast. By the time he had finished, the slower ships had caught up.

Norman Conquest of England, 1066

SCOTLAND

IRELAND

NORTH SEA

Stamford Bridge

York

Harold Hardraade's route

WALES

ENGLAND

London

Hastings

Pevensey

ISLE OF WIGHT

William's route

Saint Valéry

N

FLANDERS

English Channel

Dives

NORMANDY

BRITTANY

Invasion routes

Regional border

City

Miles

0   50   100

0   100   200

Kilometers

ATLANTIC OCEAN

The Norman fleet arrived on the English coast at mid-day on September 28. The rising tide carried them ashore at Pevensey, a coastal market town. The frightened townspeople watched them arrive, but the fyrd sent earlier to protect them had already gone home. The local people could do nothing except send a messenger to the king.

The Normans built a rough fortification at Pevensey, but they quickly decided to move on. The coastal town was not

A HEAVENLY SIGN

When a comet trailing a fiery tail moved across the skies of England in April 1066, it aroused great interest. The monk William of Jumièges and the Bayeux Tapestry both mentioned it. *The Anglo-Saxon Chronicle* recorded that "all over England there was seen a sign in the skies such as had never been seen before. Some said it was the star 'comet' which some call long-haired star; and it first appeared on the eve of the Greater Litany, that is 24 April, and so shone all the week."

Modern-day astronomers explain that this event was Halley's comet, which appears about every seventy-six years. In 1066 its appearance frightened most people. They took it as an omen of terrible things to come—a sign that God was angry and that there would be fire on earth. With the English defeat at the Battle of Hastings, it seemed to many that this prediction had been correct.

a good place for launching an attack, partly because it was not on a direct road to London. William moved his forces to Hastings. The town was about 10 miles (16 km) away as the crow flies, but it was a 30-mile (48 km) hike along a marshy track for William's men and horses. The soldiers destroyed the villages they encountered along the way.

Hastings was not much better suited for an invasion, but it was on the road to London. Also, a monastery belonging to Norman monks was located there. Perhaps William chose the spot simply because he had heard of it. At Hastings the Normans built another fortification—a simple wooden fort on a mound of earth, surrounded by a ditch—and settled in.

The Bayeux Tapestry also shows William's men working to build fortifications at Hastings.

While they waited for the English army to arrive, they stole food from the local people and destroyed much of the surrounding countryside, as conquering armies often do.

HAROLD RESPONDS

On October 1, King Harold learned that the Normans had finally arrived on the south coast. But Harold and his forces were still in York. *The Anglo-Saxon Chronicle* describes Harold's next steps: "[T]he king at once marched his army towards London with all speed; and although he knew very well that many of the better warriors in all England had fallen

Harold's army had to quickly march from Stamford Bridge to Hastings to defend England from the Norman invasion. This woodcut depicting this journey appeared in the Illustrated London News in 1882.

THE ENGLISH ARMY

The English army had two main elements—the housecarls and the fyrd. Both groups were paid. The English army traveled on horseback. However, none of the men could fight on horseback.

Housecarls wore leather jerkins and iron helmets, with long nose guards and leather flaps to cover the ears. They also carried shields. Some housecarls wielded long, Danish-style battleaxes that could knock cavalrymen off their horses. The axe men worked in teams beside other housecarls armed with swords and javelins.

The members of the fyrd at Hastings were not well armed. Many had homemade wooden shields. Their weapons included spears, short axes, hammers, scythes (tools for cutting plants), javelins, and slings for hurling stones.

in the two battles, and that half his army had not yet come in, nevertheless he did not hesitate to meet his enemy in Sussex [southeast England] as quickly as he could."

Later some people criticized Harold for acting in such haste. If he had waited, he would have had a far larger army with which to defend the country. Perhaps he hoped to surprise William with a speedy offensive, as he had Harold Hardraade. Whatever was behind his decision, King Harold and his exhausted soldiers arrived near Hastings on the night of October 13. The next morning, "King Harold . . . assembled a large army and came against him [William] at the hoary [frosted] apple-tree."

Historians estimate that Harold's force totaled about 8,800 men. William's army was slightly smaller. Harold took a position on a ridge that was easy to defend against both cavalry (soldiers on horseback) and archers. The housecarls, protected by their shields, were in the front lines, with the fyrd behind them.

The invaders lined up with the Normans in the middle, the Bretons (soldiers from Brittany) on the left, and mercenaries from France, Flanders, and other places on the right. The archers stood in front, with the foot soldiers behind them and the mounted cavalry in the rear. An experienced officer commanded each flank.

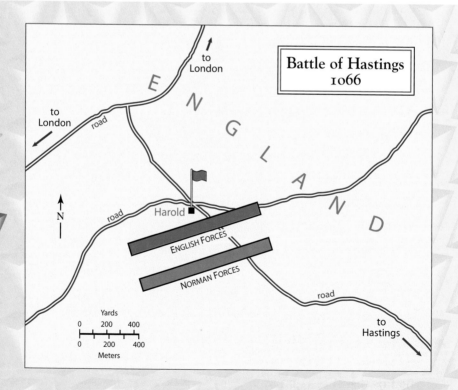

This piece of the Bayeux Tapestry shows Norman soldiers (on horses) attacking English soldiers, who have chosen the higher ground for the battle. But the English, who fought on foot, were at a disadvantage against William's knights on horseback.

The English, being on higher ground, had a better strategic position than the Normans. But the Normans had more archers (many of Harold's archers were still in the north) and well-trained knights fighting on horseback. The English were not accustomed to fighting against men on horseback. Psychologically, Harold's troops were probably the most motivated—they were defending their homeland from foreigners. Most of the Normans, on the other hand, were fighting to gain land and riches in England.

THE BATTLE

The battle began around 9:00 A.M. on October 14. William launched a quick attack. His soldiers moved in with spears and slings for hurling stones. The English replied by hurling javelins, hatchets, and stone weapons. Soon the men were

English and Norman soldiers engage in hand-to-hand combat in this American engraving of the Battle of Hastings from 1901.

engaged in hand-to-hand combat. The air was filled with the noise of metal on metal, stone on wooden shields, the shouts of the attackers, and the groans of the wounded.

Unable to break through the English line, Norman knights started to retreat in confusion. At this point some English soldiers made the mistake of chasing them. The mounted knights wheeled around and cut these isolated foot soldiers to pieces. Similar incidents happened several times during the battle. King Harold's brothers Gyrth and Leofwine died during one such episode.

William rallied his troops. As the battle continued, he ordered his archers to shoot their arrows high into the air so they would come down on the English soldiers' heads. Then the cavalry attacked. This time the exhausted and depleted English line finally faltered.

THE NORMAN ARMY

The Norman army consisted of knights, archers, and foot soldiers. In exchange for gifts of land, the knights fought for William and his barons. They also hoped to be rewarded with land and riches if Normandy were victorious. Many of the archers and foot soldiers were mercenaries, who worked for pay.

Knights wore iron helmets and armor down to their knees. Their weapons included lances, swords, and spiked clubs called maces, as well as protective shields. Foot soldiers were armed with short axes, spears, daggers, and swords. They also carried shields. Their clothes included chain mail shirts (flexible armor made of interlinking metal rings) or leather jerkins (sleeveless jackets) and iron or leather caps. Archers carried bows and arrows with an effective range of 100 yards (91.4 meters).

This German drawing shows knights in typical Norman armor at the time of the invasion of England.

Late in the battle, Harold was killed. No one is sure how he died, but the most familiar story is that an arrow struck him in the eye. Several of William's knights then reached the top of the ridge and finished off the wounded king. They stabbed him and cut off his head. As night fell, many Normans and many more English lay dead. William ordered his soldiers to stop pursuing those attempting to flee. The Battle of Hastings was over.

This etching presents a vivid picture of the Battle of Hastings. Amid a swirl of blood and violence, death and terror, an arrow strikes Harold in the eye.

THE ROAD TO LONDON

William had won a major victory, especially with King Harold's death. But he couldn't expect all opposition to disappear. His troops needed to move quickly. They had to subdue the rest of the country and crush any pockets of resistance they encountered. They also had to find food.

After resting for a few days, they advanced along the coast to the port of Dover. The town submitted without a fight. They reached the town of Canterbury before the end of October. The people of that town also surrendered. But many Norman troops contracted diarrhea there. William himself fell sick, so the Normans remained near Canterbury for a month. During this time the story of the Battle of Hastings spread across the country. Meanwhile, the witan elected Edgar the Aetheling—Edward's thirteen-year-old great nephew—as the new king of England.

The town of Winchester surrendered next, but the key to the kingdom was London. It was not only the largest and most important English town, it was also located at a strategic spot where old Roman roads converged to cross the Thames River. William did not have enough soldiers to attack London outright, so he decided to isolate it.

His troops marched to the south end of London Bridge, then to the west and north, destroying everything in their path. They wiped out whole villages outside London, including houses, fields, animals, and people.

Leading English nobles, including the archbishop of York and Edgar the Aetheling, eventually met William at a village several miles outside London. The English leaders realized that the city could not resist a siege and that the destruction of the countryside would continue. They surrendered. They gave William hostages and swore oaths of fealty to him. William promised to be a good lord to them. With few alternatives, the English leaders invited William to take the English crown.

At first William hesitated. He wanted to wait so that his wife could be crowned queen by his side. Also, at this point he controlled only a small part of England, not the whole country. But his military advisers urged him to take the

This fifteenth-century manuscript illustration shows William accepting the English crown. In the background, two buildings, including a church, are being built.

throne quickly, and he agreed. Meanwhile, he allowed his troops to continue to destroy nearby villages. William did not trust Londoners to admit him safely into the city. For protection he had his men build a fortification in the city before he stepped inside the city walls. A few days before Christmas 1066, William entered London.

A NEW KING

According to *The Anglo-Saxon Chronicle*, "Then on Christmas Day, archbishop [of York] Ealdred consecrated [William] king at Westminster. And he promised Ealdred on Christ's book and swore moreover that he would rule all his people as well as all the best of the kings before him, if they would be loyal to him."

William's coronation ceremony at Westminster Abbey was similar to those of earlier English kings. But there was one difference: this time, church leaders asked those present, in English and in French, whether they would recognize William as king. When the crowd shouted its agreement, the soldiers outside the church thought there was trouble inside. They began to set fire to neighboring houses. Despite the commotion, the coronation service was completed. William, the duke of Normandy, had finally become King William I of England. He also became known as William the Conqueror.

CHAPTER SIX
AFTER THE BATTLE

All the same [William] laid taxes on people very severely
and then went in spring to Normandy. . . . And Bishop
Odo and Earl William stayed behind and built castles far
and wide throughout this country, and distressed the
wretched folk, and always after that it grew much worse.
May the end be good when God wills.

—The Anglo-Saxon Chronicle, *1100s*

As 1066 drew to a close, the newly crowned King
William I faced many challenges. The Normans controlled
only southern England. The north, as well as neighboring
Wales and Scotland, were enemy territories. King Harold's
sons were still alive to challenge William. Edgar the
Aetheling had many supporters, and the Scandinavians
were not about to give up their interests in England.
William brought extra troops from Normandy to keep

PENANCE

Church leaders required William and his followers to do penance, or express sorrow and regret, for the killings they had committed during the conquest. In this way they would be saved from going to hell. As part of their penance, some soldiers gave money to the poor or paid for the construction of a church. As his penance William built a monastery, Battle Abbey, on the spot where Harold had died.

control in England. Meanwhile, he also had to maintain his power in Normandy.

William went back to Normandy in the spring of 1067. He left his friend William FitzOsbern and his half brother Odo in charge of England. During that year rebellions broke out in several regions. But the fighting did not last long, and many more towns submitted to William's rule. Returning to England, William defeated Harold's sons, then celebrated Easter 1068 at the town of Winchester, England. His wife, Matilda, came to England and was crowned queen in May.

A HEAVY HAND

Up to this point, resistance to the Normans had been mild. But then the new king started giving English lands to his friends and supporters. He seized land from the Godwin family and others who had fought with Harold. He imposed high taxes on everyone. By 1069 the uneasy peace between the English and their new king had broken down.

A serious resistance movement grew in the north. Danish forces, allied with the English, arrived at the Humber River. They sparked a major uprising against the Normans. In Scotland, King Malcolm III threw his support behind Edgar the Aetheling. The combined threat from the Danes, Edgar's supporters, and the Scots led William to take extreme measures.

He led his troops to York, destroying all the land they passed through. William's soldiers killed people and slaughtered animals. They destroyed houses, agricultural fields, and even seeds for the next growing season. They ruined monasteries and churches and burned the city of York. Then they moved west across the mountains, despite terrible winter weather, and crushed resistance there. The Danes realized that their allies in England had been defeated. They agreed to a truce and sailed for home. William's cruel methods were effective. By the spring of 1070, the main resistance to his rule had been crushed.

William tried to persuade the English that his rule was lawful. He insisted that he was Edward's true successor and

An eighteenth-century English engraving of King Malcolm III of Scotland that it was Harold who had stolen the crown. William did manage to amass some support in his new kingdom. Some English thanes helped him administer the country. Moreover, English church leaders supported him because he promised to help the church.

In 1072 William, determined to deal with a renewed threat from Scotland, launched a two-pronged invasion of Scotland, by sea and by land. King Malcolm decided to negotiate rather than fight. He recognized William as his lord, and he withdrew his support of Edgar. To establish his authority, William built castles in strategic locations in the north and along the border with Wales.

PART-TIME KING

William had conquered England with relative ease. As king he owned vast amounts of land in England. But he never really felt comfortable there. He never learned English. He spent much of his time in Normandy, where problems with hostile neighbors continued. He also had problems within his own family. He fought with Odo and with his oldest son, Robert, who challenged him for power in Normandy.

Robert, eldest son of William the Conqueror

CASTLES

One of the first things the Norman invaders did after an English town or region surrendered was to build a castle. Many went up very quickly. The invaders forced English laborers to help with the construction. In towns they simply demolished any houses that stood in the way. The castles allowed the Normans to control the surrounding area and served as bases for further advance through the countryside.

Not long after the Battle of Hastings, the Normans created a network of castles at the mouths of rivers along the southern English coast. This network enabled William to easily send messengers to Normandy and to bring soldiers and supplies across the channel. By the end of William's reign, more than eighty Norman castles towered over the English countryside.

The most common type of castle was called a motte and bailey. First, workers dug a ditch in the shape of a circle or oval. In one

William did love to hunt in England. He created a vast forest, called the New Forest, by planting trees on former farmland. Anyone caught hunting the king's deer in the king's forest faced severe punishment. The English deeply resented William's hunting laws and saw them as a symbol of his greed.

The Danes threatened to invade England again in 1085. This time William brought a large mercenary force

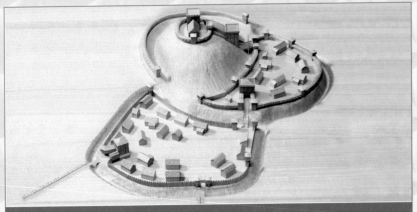

This is a twentieth-century British model of a twelfth-century Norman motte and bailey castle. The keep is on top of a large hill, called a motte. Additional buildings stand inside the bailey.

part of the circle, they piled dirt into a large mound called a motte. They constructed a strong wooden building, called a keep, on top of the motte. They also erected a palisade, a tall wooden fence, inside the ditch. The enclosed area between the motte and the palisade was called the bailey. Years later, the Normans replaced many of their original timber castles with stone structures.

from Normandy to protect the country. The Danish invasion never occurred. But William worried about paying for the troops he needed to have at the ready in both Normandy and England. He discussed the problem with his English advisers at court that Christmas. They decided to carry out a massive survey to evaluate the kingdom's resources, the value of its land, and the wealth of its inhabitants. According to *The Anglo-Saxon Chronicle*, "King William caused the whole of England to be surveyed, how much land each of his barons possessed, how many . . . knights, how many ploughs . . . how many ani-

THE DOMESDAY BOOK

William wanted to know the value of his English kingdom, so he ordered that a huge survey be done. Officials divided the country into seven regions and assigned several commissioners to each. In each village or estate, the commissioners asked a set of questions. They determined the total amount of land, how many serfs and slaves lived on the land, how much of the land was woodland, how many animals lived there, what types of buildings there were, and so forth. When the commissioners returned to London, they combined their findings with earlier records. The first draft of the survey, later called the Domesday Book, was completed in August 1086. It contained records for some 13,418 settlements. The 413-page document was handwritten in Latin on sheepskin.

Although the Domesday Book provided a unique record of the time, it had several shortcomings. It left out the cities of London and Winchester, and it omitted four northern counties. It listed only the heads of households rather than all individuals and did not record people who lived in castles, monasteries, or nunneries. Nevertheless, some historians consider this massive undertaking to be William's most important contribution to history.

mals and what livestock everybody had from the highest to the lowest in all his kingdom, and what rent could be obtained from every estate." The survey became known as the Domesday Book.

The book acquired its name because people thought a similar kind of accounting would happen on doomsday, the day of God's last judgment predicted by the Bible. The original Domesday Book is displayed at the National Archives in London. Almost all the places it mentions can still be found on maps of England and Wales, although some have changed their names since the eleventh century.

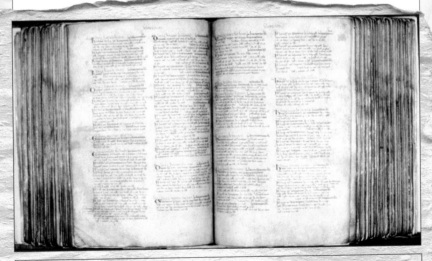

The original Domesday Book (above) is held at the British National Archives in London. The text is available on the Internet at http://www .nationalarchives.gov.uk/domesday/. Historians and others can search the online text to learn about life and people in medieval England.

ASSESSING WILLIAM THE CONQUEROR

An entry in *The Anglo-Saxon Chronicle* for 1087 summed up William the Conqueror's life this way:

This king William of whom we speak was a very wise man, and very powerful and more worshipful and stronger than any predecessor of his had been. He was gentle to the good men who loved God, and stern beyond all measure to those people who resisted his will. . . . Also, he was very dignified: three times each year he wore his crown, as often as he was in England. At Easter he wore it at Winchester, at Whitsuntide at Westminster, and at Christmas at Gloucester, and then there were with him all the powerful men over all England, archbishops and bishops, abbots and earls, thanes and knights. Also, he was a very stern and violent man, so that no one dared do anything contrary to his will.

NORMAN KINGS

In 1087, during a campaign against the French, William and his troops attacked and burned the town of Mantes, not far from Paris. William was injured in an accident while riding through the burning town. He died several weeks later. His death raised two central questions: Would William's heirs be able to establish a lasting dynasty (ruling family) in England? And would England and Normandy continue to share a ruler?

William and Matilda had three adult sons. William had decided many years earlier that his eldest son, Robert, would succeed him as duke of Normandy. But then Robert sided with his father's enemies in Normandy, so William changed his mind. As the king lay dying, he sent his middle son, William—nicknamed Rufus (meaning "red") because of his ruddy complexion—to England. William Rufus carried a letter from his father. It instructed Lanfranc, archbishop of Canterbury, to crown him King William II.

William II was a strong and outspoken leader. In 1100 he died in a hunting accident in the New Forest. His younger brother, Henry, seized the opportunity and was crowned king three days later. King Henry I had been born in England and spoke English. Many magnates supported him. He was a cruel man, but he was also educated, energetic, and a good administrator.

There was peace in England during most of Henry I's reign. Henry married Matilda, the daughter of King Malcolm of Scotland and his wife, Margaret, a sister of Edgar the Aetheling. Henry and Matilda had a son and a daughter. After the son drowned in the English Channel, Henry chose his daughter, also named Matilda, to succeed him. The magnates swore loyalty to her, although they did not like the idea of a female leader.

This illustration from the Golden Book of Saint Albans (1380) shows Matilda holding a legal document.

THE KINGS OF ENGLAND 802–1189

NAME	REIGN
Egbert	802–839
Ethelwulf	839–858
Ethelbald	858–860
Ethelbert	860–865?
Ethelred I	865?–871
Alfred the Great	871–899
Edward the Elder	899–924
Athelstan	924–939
Edmund I	939–946
Edred	946–955
Eadwig	955–959
Edgar	959–975

When Henry died suddenly in 1135, Matilda was unable to take the crown. She was in Anjou, France, where her husband, Geoffrey Plantagenet, was a young count. Her cousin Stephen (William the Conqueror's grandson) took advantage of the opportunity. He crossed the English Channel as soon as he heard of Henry's death and seized the English crown.

Although King Stephen I was charming and brave, he had difficulty controlling the kingdom and attracting loyal

Edward the Martyr	975–978?
Ethelred II	978?–1016
Edmund II	1016
Canute	1016–1035
Harold I	1035–1040
Hardecanute	1040–1042
Edward the Confessor	1042–1066
Harold II (Harold Godwinson)	1066
William I, the Conqueror	1066–1087
William II	1087–1100
Henry I	1100–1135
Stephen I	1135–1154
Henry II	1154–1189

followers. In 1139 Matilda invaded England to try to claim the throne. Many years of civil war followed, as Stephen's forces fought Matilda's troops. Finally, Stephen and Matilda negotiated a peace treaty. According to the agreement, Stephen would remain king until his death, whereupon Matilda's son Henry would inherit the throne.

When Stephen died in 1154, the throne passed to Henry as planned. For the first time in a century, no one contested

This thirteenth-century illustration from Matthew Paris's Historia Anglorum (The History of the English) shows the first four Norman kings (clockwise from top left: William the Conqueror, William Rufus, Stephen, and Henry I).

the succession. Henry became King Henry II of England. At the time he already ruled Normandy, Anjou, and Maine on the European continent. In taking over England, he became the most powerful monarch in Europe. His lands stretched from Scotland to the Pyrenees Mountains (in modern-day southwestern France). The son of Matilda and Geoffrey Plantagenet, Henry was the first in a long line of Plantagenet kings. The Norman dynasty was over. The Plantagenet kings ruled England uncontested until 1485.

CHAPTER SEVEN
A BLENDED SOCIETY

At this time [circa 1070] by the grace of God peace reined over England; and a degree of security returned to its inhabitants. . . . English and Normans were living peacefully together in boroughs, towns and cities, and were intermarrying with each other. You could see many villages or town markets filled with displays of French wares and merchandise, and observe the English, who had previously seemed contemptible to the French in their native dress, completely transformed by foreign fashions.

—*Ordericus Vitalis*, The Ecclesiastical History, c. 1070

Fewer than twenty-five thousand Normans settled in England following the conquest. Compared to England's total population of about 1.5 million, this was a small amount. But these newcomers had a big impact on English government, language, and society. The conquest also brought political changes. Before the conquest, England was closely linked to Scandinavia but not to the rest of Europe. Afterward, England's political focus shifted to Normandy and continental Europe.

England also enjoyed a period of economic growth after the conquest. The population expanded slowly. Towns grew, especially London. Craftspeople such as carpenters, brewers, leatherworkers, weavers, goldsmiths, and masons (stoneworkers) prospered. Coastal ports flourished as England exported wool and herring to the continent. English merchants imported silver from Germany to make coins and stone from Normandy to build great new churches. The conquest also exposed England to new sources of knowledge. Norman bishops and abbots filled church and monastery libraries with new books from mainland Europe.

At first the Norman newcomers did not blend well into English society. But over time Norman settlers and their descendants came to look upon themselves as English

The English economy prospered after the Norman conquest. This image shows two masons laying the stones for Clifford's Tower at Saint Albans cathedral in the late eleventh century. This illustration is from a fourteenth-century book called the Lives of the Offas by Matthew Paris.

rather than Norman. Intermarriage, especially among small landowners, servants, merchants, and other middle-class people, helped blur distinctions between the English and the Normans.

THE NEW NOBILITY

One of the biggest changes in England after the conquest was the complete replacement of the nobility. Many English nobles died in the battles of 1066 or in the rebellions that followed. Those who survived found themselves much worse off than before. For the most part, William seized their lands and sent them into exile.

Meanwhile, many men who had signed up to follow William across the channel expected payment in the form of

DOCUMENTING THE DIFFERENCE

The Domesday survey showed how extensively Normans replaced the English nobility. According to the survey, in 1086, twenty years after the conquest, the king and queen directly owned about 17 percent of the land in England. Norman barons controlled 48.5 percent. The church controlled 26.5 percent. Another 2.5 percent belonged to government staff and officials. Only 5.5 percent was still in the hands of English magnates who had owned land before the war. However, under new landownership laws, the king officially owned all the land in England.

land and high government posts in England. William did reward them in these ways. Some Norman barons became English magnates. They traveled back and forth across the channel regularly. Some Norman lords married Englishwomen, thereby strengthening their claims to lands William had given them. Large Norman landholders often subdivided their estates, giving portions of land to their relatives and followers. But under Norman rules of landownership, all land ultimately belonged to the king—all other landowners, including barons, were merely the king's tenants.

Many villagers hated their new Norman lords. The lords spoke a different language and practiced different customs. Some treated their serfs harshly. In turn, some English people rebelled against their Norman lords. To protect themselves, barons built private castles. The countryside took on a new look. Castles, surrounded by walls and moats and protected by armed guards, replaced the old Anglo-Saxon manor houses.

Durham Castle, constructed beginning in 1076, is a typical Norman-era English castle. The strong central fortress is called a keep.

COURT OFFICIALS

The people who ran the king's household were very powerful, and new positions developed under the Norman kings. The chamberlain, who looked after the king's bedchamber, was a central figure. Much of the king's wealth was kept in his chamber, and the man responsible for this treasure was called the treasurer. The chancellor wrote legal documents for the king. As written documents became more important in governing the country, the chancellor's importance increased. Because a Norman king was often away on the continent, he needed an official to run England in his absence. This official was called the justiciar. Another new position was the exchequer. His main role was to see that the king received all the money that was owed to him.

LAW AND ORDER

King William I conquered a strong and wealthy kingdom with an advanced system of government. England had an efficient tax system. Its monetary system was better than any in northwestern Europe. Rather than trying to change England's government, William used it to his advantage.

Once the initial rebellions against him had died down, William succeeded in maintaining law and order in England. *The Anglo-Saxon Chronicle* noted, "Amongst other things the good security he made in this country is not to be forgotten—so that any honest man could travel over his kingdom without injury with his bosom full of gold; and no one dared strike [kill] another, however much wrong he had done him."

William allowed the English to retain their own legal traditions. English courts continued to follow customary laws, as well as the laws of King Canute. Traveling judges, who worked for the king, visited local courts to hear cases involving serious crimes and land disputes. Meanwhile, barons settled differences in their own courts, according to Norman traditions. In the twelfth century, the two threads of English and Norman laws began to come together as English common law. This body of law is the basis for laws still used in the United States, Canada, and other countries with historic ties to Great Britain.

The Normans brought new military traditions to England. They, like most Europeans, fought on horseback. The English had never fought on horseback. But after the conquest, a new generation of English knights learned to do so. The military also increased in importance. William and his successors needed a large, trained army, especially for campaigns in Normandy. The barons needed soldiers and guards for protection. With the creation of a large new army, England's fyrd, the old poorly trained and ill-equipped militia, disappeared.

CHANGES TO THE CHURCH

William had led the invasion of England under the pope's banner and promoted it as a campaign to reform the English church. To carry out his reforms, William replaced the archbishop of Canterbury, the head of the English church, with a

Norman monk named Lanfranc. Normans eventually replaced most other church officials. These new leaders tried to discourage priests from marrying and forbade simony (the sale of positions in the church).

Like almost everyone in the Middle Ages, the Normans were extremely religious. Under Norman rule, more and more people in England decided to live in monasteries and

LIFE IN A MONASTERY

Monastery life in Norman England was strictly regulated. The year was divided into three seasons: winter, Lent (the weeks leading up to Easter), and summer. In winter the day's only meal was eaten at 2:00 P.M. During Lent monks ate at 6:00 P.M. There were two meals a day in summer, eaten at noon and 6:00 P.M. Most of the time, monks were not supposed to speak, so they could better connect with their inner selves and with God.

Monks slept in their robes and shoes. They attended the first of many daily church services at 2:00 A.M. in an unheated church. At around 8:00 A.M. the monks washed. Then the rule of silence was relaxed for several hours while the monks worked. Those with writing and drawing skills copied and illustrated books. Others looked after land and animals, tended the sick in the infirmary, hosted travelers who visited the monastery, rehearsed with the choir, or taught children who came to the monastery for an education. In keeping with Christian doctrine, monks also nunneries and devote their lives to religion. The Cistercians, a new order of monks that originated in France, built new monasteries in England after the conquest. Cistercian monks lived very simple lives. They wore only rough woolen robes. They followed strict rules that forbade them to eat meat and forbade them to talk to each other for much of the day.

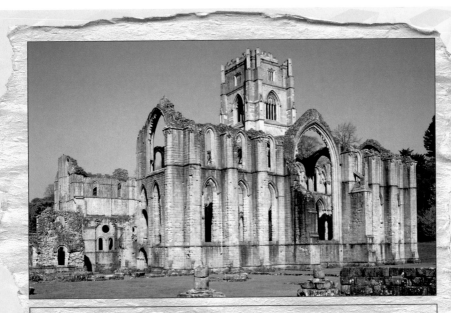

This monastery, known as Fountains Abbey, was built under Norman rule in Yorkshire, England, by the Cistercian order.

fed and housed poor people who were unable to care for themselves. Hired servants did much of the cleaning, cooking, gardening, and other chores at monasteries.

NEW ARCHITECTURE

The Norman impact on architecture was in plain view across the English countryside. A construction boom occurred as the Normans built imposing new castles, manor houses, monasteries, nunneries, and churches. Some structures were built of stone imported from France. Others were made with local building materials.

Norman-appointed bishops tore down many Anglo-Saxon churches and built new ones. Magnificent new cathedrals (large churches that serve as headquarters for bishops) appeared in towns such as Canterbury, Winchester, and Durham. The new churches were constructed in a style unique to Norman England, with thick walls that gave a solid appearance, as well as rounded arches and square towers. Skilled Norman masons, working with axes, carved sculptures and geometric patterns into the stone exteriors. Inside, Norman-era churches had long naves (central halls) and large round columns. Metalsmiths created engraved gold or silver religious objects, while artists plastered and painted the walls. Church doors featured ornate iron keyholes, hinges, and padlocks.

OUT WITH THE OLD ENGLISH

Before the conquest Old English was the language of both kings and commoners. Monks wrote legal documents, poetry, and other works in Old English and sometimes Latin. But the situation changed rapidly after 1066. The new Norman nobility spoke French and looked down on those who spoke English. English became the language of the common people, while French became the language of government and business.

THE TOWER OF LONDON

The Tower of London is a group of stone buildings on the Thames River. The tower *(below)* was built as a fortified palace for William the Conqueror. Construction began in 1067. The original building was made of wood. Ten years later the Normans began to rebuild the central tower, or White Tower, using stone. Three stories high, with walls 15 feet (4.5 m) thick, the tower was completed in 1097. Originally, the ground floor was a prison and storage area. A great hall, chapel, and private quarters for the royal family were located above. Additional buildings were added over time. In modern times the Tower of London complex serves as a museum.

Legal, church, and scholarly documents were written in French or Latin.

Many English people became bilingual. They had to learn French to succeed in business. Some gave their children French names, such as William, Henry, and Richard. French words quickly entered the English language after the conquest. *Castle, jury, duke, flowers, courage,* and *season* are all words with French origins.

Over time French-speaking Normans intermarried with the English and loosened their ties with France. When this happened Normans and their descendants began to speak English. By the late 1300s, English had again taken over as the language of business and government. However, it was a Frenchified version of English, later known as Middle English.

LAND AND MARRIAGE

In Norman England all land ultimately belonged to the king. And since marriage was closely linked to land (nobles married their children to one another to increase their landholdings), the king had to approve all marriages within noble families. Any nobleman who married without the king's approval had to pay a fine and risked losing his land. Similarly, lords had to approve the marriages of their tenants and knights.

The new laws greatly reduced women's rights in Norman England. Women could no longer own property or choose their own husbands. If a nobleman died before his eldest son reached adulthood, his land went back to the king, and the king became the guardian of the nobleman's wife and children. He arranged marriages for them. If a woman with land married, her husband acquired control over her land. If she remarried after the death of her husband, her new husband acquired her property. If a widow was determined not to remarry, she had to pay a large fee to the king for the right to remain single.

THE LOWER CLASSES

In some ways, life for the lower classes did not change much after the Norman Conquest. Most people still worked as farmers. Others were craftspeople, knights, merchants, or servants. The destinies of slaves (the Domesday Book listed twenty-five thousand) improved after the Norman Conquest. Slavery gradually disappeared in postconquest England, partly because the Norman-led church preached against Christians enslaving other Christians. Many former slaves became serfs or free farmers.

THE CONQUEST REMEMBERED

Many both Normans and English have written about king William for different reasons; the former have praised him to excess, lauding both his good and bad deeds to the skies; the latter, out of national hatred, have heaped upon their ruler undeserved reproach.

—*William of Malmesbury,* The Deeds of the Kings of the English, *1125*

The year 1066 has become one of the most familiar moments in British history. In modern times, the English proudly point out that the Normans were the last people to successfully invade their island. Even though the English lost the battle, they relish it as a pivotal moment in their history. The dramatic Battle of Hastings has captured the national imagination. While few Britons are familiar with the military details, everyone knows the story of the arrow in King Harold's eye.

Each October, tourists flock to Hastings. There they watch history buffs dressed up in medieval costumes reenact the battle. Books on the subject appear frequently as modern historians analyze the conquest anew. Dozens of websites describe the personalities involved, the events leading up to 1066, and the consequences of the conquest. Some sites are designed for schoolchildren, others for adults. Most feature rich illustrations taken from medieval sources.

More than three thousand performers reenact the Battle of Hastings in October 2006. Reenactors carefully research the battle. They use weapons and costumes that look just like those used in 1066.

This statue of William the Conqueror stands in front of the Houses of Parliament in London.

Statues of William the Conqueror stand in places of honor in front of the Houses of Parliament in London, in Westminster Hall (the oldest part of a palace built by William's son William Rufus), and other locations in the United Kingdom and France. The English also remember King Harold. Modern history books credit him as a brave commander, both at Stamford Bridge and at Hastings. Tourists visit the stone marker where he died at Battle Abbey. They also visit Waltham Abbey, north of London, where he is said to be buried (although new archaeological evidence suggests he is buried elsewhere). Since 2003

[see below]

This statue of William the Conqueror stands in front of the Houses of Parliament in London.

Statues of William the Conqueror stand in places of honor in front of the Houses of Parliament in London, in Westminster Hall (the oldest part of a palace built by William's son William Rufus), and other locations in the United Kingdom and France. The English also remember King Harold. Modern history books credit him as a brave commander, both at Stamford Bridge and at Hastings. Tourists visit the stone marker where he died at Battle Abbey. They also visit Waltham Abbey, north of London, where he is said to be buried (although new archaeological evidence suggests he is buried elsewhere). Since 2003

Waltham Abbey has been the site of King Harold Day. This annual festival features craft demonstrations, weaponry displays, medieval food, and music.

For historians the short-term impact of the Norman conquest of England is clear. This event ended the rule of the Anglo-Saxon kings and put a new dynasty of Norman rulers on the throne of England. It created one of the most powerful monarchies in Europe. It linked the island kingdom to the continent, especially to France, while virtually cutting off England's ties with Scandinavia.

Under the Normans, England's nobility changed and the church changed. The newcomers brought new influences in architecture, the military, and social customs. The conquest had one of its most significant effects on the English language. The Normans introduced a great many French words into English. Eventually, however, English prevailed over French.

The English bitterly resented the conquest at first. They disliked the Norman army of occupation, the ruthless way the new king dealt with rebels, and the foreign lords who displaced the Anglo-Saxon magnates. But during the first century after the conquest, both the Anglo-Saxons and the Normans realized that the newcomers were there to stay, and they mingled and married.

While the Normans initially changed England, England also changed the Norman settlers. It was not long before they started referring to themselves as English. Subject to common laws and rulers, they shared the same Christian beliefs and enjoyed similar traditions. They also shared a common Viking ancestry.

English noblemen and noblewomen during the Norman period as drawn in the nineteenth century. The upper classes changed most of all after the Norman Conquest, with new styles of clothing, new words, and new social systems brought from mainland Europe.

The Anglo-Saxons had laid solid foundations in England. Spurred by the threat of Viking invasions, kings such as Alfred the Great had united warring people under one centralized government and created systems of justice, finance, and defense. The Normans, who were smart imitators, maintained and built on these government institutions without making radical changes. The result was one of the most sophisticated governments of the time.

As for King William I, after he had been on the throne for a few years, he acted as though he was the legitimate successor of Edward the Confessor. Both the Bayeux Tapestry and William's biographers emphasized Edward's promise that William would succeed him and accused Harold of breaking his oath to help the duke to become king of England. William's biographers also treated Harold as though he had not been a rightful ruler. Although Harold ran a functioning government for nine months in 1066, William's backers referred to him as Count Harold rather than King Harold II.

Yet in the long run, it seems that William lost the propaganda battle, for history remembers William as the foreign conqueror of England. He won the kingdom in battle, and he harshly repressed rebellion. As a result, the English did not view him as the good lord he promised to be. Although history accords him respect for his achievements, he never won the hearts of the English people.

One thousand years later, historians still debate what happened in the years leading up to 1066. Some people doubt that Edward promised William the throne, while others believe that Harold broke his oath. Even in modern times, the memory of the conquest is painful for some English people. They feel the Norman conquerors oppressed the English. Others say the hardships the English experienced after 1066 helped them adapt to new circumstances. They see the long-term benefits of the events of 1066.

Historians may never agree about all the consequences of the conquest. But they do agree that it was a pivotal moment in history.

PRIMARY SOURCE RESEARCH

To learn about historical events, people study many sources, such as books, websites, newspaper articles, photographs, and paintings. These sources can be separated into two general categories—primary sources and secondary sources.

A primary source is a record of an eyewitness or someone living during the time being studied. Primary sources often provide firsthand accounts about a person or event. Examples include diaries, letters, autobiographies, speeches, newspapers, and oral history interviews. Libraries, archives, historical societies, and museums often have primary sources available on-site or on the Internet.

A secondary source is published information that was researched, collected, and written or created after the event in question. Authors and artists who create secondary sources use primary sources and other secondary sources in their research. Secondary sources include history books, novels, biographies, movies, documentaries, and magazines. Libraries and museums are filled with secondary sources.

After finding primary and secondary sources, authors and historians must evaluate them. They may ask questions such as: Who created this document? What is this person's point of view? What biases might this person have? How trustworthy is this document? Just because a person was an eyewitness to an event does not mean that person recorded the whole truth about that event. For example, a soldier describing a battle might depict only the heroic actions of his unit and only the brutal behavior of the enemy. An account from a soldier on the opposing side might portray the same battle very differently. When sources disagree, researchers must decide through additional study which explanation makes the most sense. For this reason, historians consult a variety of primary and secondary sources. Then they can draw their own conclusions.

The Pivotal Moments in History series takes readers on a journey to important junctures in history that shaped our modern world. Authors researched each event using both primary and secondary sources, an approach that enhances readers' awareness of the complexities of the materials and helps bring to life the rich stories from which we draw our understanding of our shared history.

THE REMNANTS OF HISTORY

Modern historians researching the Norman Conquest face several difficulties figuring out what happened. For one thing, few people could read and write in 1066. There were no reporters to cover political events or war correspondents to interview soldiers who fought at Hastings. Most news passed by word-of-mouth from one individual to another. It traveled no faster than a messenger on horseback.

Writers at the time of the conquest rarely had firsthand knowledge of the topics they covered. For instance, the monks who compiled *The Anglo-Saxon Chronicle* had not witnessed the events they documented. They simply wrote down what they had heard from others. And in the period before the invention of the printing press (it wasn't used until the 1400s), monks who hand-copied documents sometimes made mistakes.

Many documents from the era of the Norman Conquest have been lost or destroyed. Some were damaged in fires, floods, and wars. In a few cases, only sections of original documents remain. Henry VIII, who ruled England in the early sixteenth century, broke with the church in Rome. He shut down English monasteries and their libraries. Some manuscripts were destroyed on the spot. Others were sold for their paper.

DOCUMENTING THE CONQUEST

As for the Battle of Hastings, a few historians did record the event. Much of their information came by word-of-mouth. Details and accuracy were probably lost along the way. One of the most complete descriptions of the events of 1066 comes from a version of *The Anglo-Saxon Chronicle* known as the Florence of Worcester version. The author of this version was either a monk named Florence who died in 1118 or another monk, John of Worcester, who may have continued the work Florence started. Whoever the writer was, he based his account on other documents, especially one written by an Irish-born monk named Marianus Scotus. Piecing together documents this way was common in the Middle Ages.

Some people who created documents about the Norman Conquest wrote them as propaganda. Propaganda is writing and other material designed to influence people's beliefs. In the case of the Norman Conquest, Anglo-Saxons produced propaganda, and Normans produced propaganda—each side trying to convince people of its own point of view. On the Anglo-Saxon side, Edith, wife of King Edward, hired someone to write a biography of her husband. Edith was a member of the powerful Godwin family, and the book was biased toward the family. *The Anglo-Saxon Chronicle*, another English source, is also biased toward different families and factions.

Norman sources include the Bayeux Tapestry, which illustrates the Norman Conquest in pictures. William's half brother Odo probably had the tapestry created. The large embroidered work shows William as a brave and rightful leader. A history of the Norman dukes, written by a monk named William of Jumièges in 1070 and 1071, also supports William's claim to the throne of England.

The Deeds of William II, Duke of Normandy, is yet another primary source about the Normans. Its author was William

A page of William of Jumièges's work, The Deeds of the Norman Dukes. *The illustration shows Jumièges offering his book to William the Conqueror.*

of Poitiers, who worked for William. William of Poitiers's original manuscript was lost. A surviving edition, copied in 1619, covers the period 1035 to 1068. Although William of Poitiers wrote this biography to justify William's conquest of England, modern historians nevertheless regard it as a valuable document.

The first professional historians to look back on this period lived in the twelfth century. Between 1109 and 1141, a monk named Ordericus Vitalis wrote *The Ecclesiastical History*, a thirteen-volume history of the church and the Normans. He based much of his research about the conquest period on William of Jumièges' earlier book, *The Deeds of the Norman Dukes*.

Another monk, William of Malmesbury, produced a number of well-researched history books, including *The Deeds of the Kings of the English*, written in 1125. Henry of Huntingdon's *The History of the English People 1000–1154* is

This illustration comes from Henry of Huntingdon's twelfth-century English history text.

another source from this period. The author had access to libraries and documents that have since disappeared, as well as to oral histories (stories passed along by word-of-mouth).

Other sources of information about the conquest period include poems, illustrations, letters, and legal documents such as wills and land transactions. The Domesday Book is a valuable source of information about England after the conquest. Depending on who wrote them, materials from the period were written in Latin, Old English, or French. Scholars have translated the documents into modern English.

PROBLEMS FOR MODERN READERS

Delving into primary sources requires a bit of extra effort. Even though the works had been translated into English, the language, as it was written and spoken hundreds of years ago, feels unfamiliar. Some accounts expressed unfamiliar attitudes. For example, William of Poitiers described William of Normandy as "hurling himself upon [his enemies], he terrified them with slaughter." The writer meant these words as glowing praise. But it's hard to imagine modern political commentators in the United States praising government leaders for ruthlessly killing their enemies.

Henry of Huntingdon wrote about the English: "[B]ecause of the enormity of their crimes—for they were not only at all times bent on slaughter and treachery, but also continually given over to drunkenness and the neglect of the Lord's house [the church]—an unforeseen lordship would come upon [the English] from France." Henry of

Huntingdon was convinced that the conquest was God's punishment of the English. Modern historians disagree. They think that Harold's forces lost because they were depleted and exhausted after the battle at Stamford Bridge and their long march. Even so, it's important to consider Henry of Huntingdon's opinion. It gives us a window into what the people of the time were thinking. People in the Middle Ages viewed the world through religious eyes. They believed that God regularly intervened in their lives.

THE BIG PICTURE

In addition to written sources, historians study artifacts, or everyday objects, from Anglo-Saxon and Norman England. These objects include coins, jewelry, pottery, and weapons.

This Anglo-Saxon sword was found in the Thames River. It dates approximately to the era of the Norman Conquest.

They provide additional clues about the daily lives of royalty and ordinary citizens. For example, pieces of German pottery found in English port towns indicate that trade was common in Anglo-Saxon England. Illustrations, too, such as the Bayeux Tapestry and illuminated manuscripts, also offer insights into the Anglo-Saxon and Norman worlds. By combining information from English legal documents, Norman documents, illustrations, and other artifacts of the time, historians can begin to put together the story of William's conquest of England.

But many questions about the Norman Conquest will never be answered. The medieval documents that might have answered them have disappeared. Maybe they never existed in the first place. But perhaps the remaining questions are part of this story's appeal. They add a touch of mystery to a tale that is already full of intrigue.

PRIMARY SOURCE DOCUMENT: THE BAYEUX TAPESTRY

The Bayeux Tapestry is unique. It is both a work of art and an important historical document that tells the story of William, Harold, and the Norman Conquest of England.

The tapestry is a series of eight linen rectangles, stitched together to make one long strip. It features a series of illustrations, embroidered in mostly brown, red, blue, and green wool. A short description accompanies each illustration. Pictures of animals and familiar fables fill the borders along the top and bottom of the tapestry.

The first sequence of images shows Harold Godwinson sailing across the English Channel in 1064. After the count of Ponthieu's soldiers arrest Harold, the duke of Normandy frees him. Then Harold accompanies Duke William on a military expedition. Harold swears to support William's claim to the English throne and returns home. After Edward the Confessor dies, Harold succeeds to the throne. The tapestry ends with scenes of the Battle of Hastings and Harold's death.

Several facts lead historians to believe that Odo, half brother to William the Conqueror, ordered the tapestry made. First, Odo and three of his followers appear prominently in the tapestry, although the three followers did not play important roles in the conquest. Second, the completed tapestry hung in the cathedral at Bayeux, where Odo was bishop, when it opened in 1077.

After the conquest, Odo became earl of Kent in southeastern England. The tapestry was probably embroidered in an abbey in Canterbury, Kent. The Anglo-Saxons had a long tradition of illustrating manuscripts, and the tapestry displays an Anglo-Saxon artistic style. For historians, it would be interesting to compare the Bayeux Tapestry to other English tapestries from the era, but no such tapestries survive.

The Bayeux Tapestry was created very soon after the conquest, at the request of someone close to the events. It is a primary source document, and historians consider it a reliable historical record. But it is also a piece of propaganda that tells the story Odo wanted to tell. It emphasizes William's preparations to invade England and portrays him as a great leader. But the tapestry is also fair to Harold. Later Norman accounts of the conquest did not even note that Harold had been crowned king of England. The Bayeux Tapestry depicts Harold as king—and as a brave soldier who died a hero.

The tapestry focuses on an event that raised an important moral issue for people in the eleventh century. That issue was the oath Harold made to support William's claim to the English throne. According to the tapestry, not only did Harold make this promise, he swore it on sacred relics. By accepting the crown after King Edward's death, Harold broke his oath. To many people in Normandy, that deed meant Harold could not be England's rightful ruler. William had an excuse to take the crown by force.

The text that accompanies the illustrations is in Latin, which was commonly used in Normandy at the time. But some of the spellings, such as the name Eadwardus (Edward), reflect an Anglo-Saxon influence. The spelling of Willelm (William) is a mixture of Old English and French.

The tapestry tells its story in a clear, concise manner, although in one spot it reverses the sequence of events. It shows King Edward being buried before he dies. Nevertheless, the people of Bayeux were familiar with the events of the Norman Conquest and would have had no difficulty understanding the story as presented.

The tapestry tells modern historians a great deal about life in this period. For example, it shows the type of weapons soldiers used and how they built their ships and fortifications. It also shows servants preparing food and Normans sitting down to enjoy a feast. However, no one knows how accurate these illustrations are or whether they were done from memory or imagination.

The tapestry has survived almost one thousand years. For much of that time it was folded up and stored away. The caretakers at the Bayeux Cathedral displayed it for only a week or so each year. In this way it survived fires and wars. During the French Revolution, in the late 1700s, someone used the tapestry as a wagon cover. A lawyer managed to save it.

The French general and emperor Napoleon moved the tapestry to Paris in 1803. To rally his people with the tale of victory over the English, he put it on public display as he prepared to invade England. The tapestry was returned to Bayeux around 1842. For safety it spent part of World War II (1939–1945) in the basement of the Louvre Museum in Paris.

Over time, sections of the fabric have deteriorated. Various hands have made repairs. The first section of the tapestry is badly damaged, and the last section is missing entirely. Each rip, missing letter, or imperfect repair raises questions about what information may be missing or what crucial detail may have been changed.

In the 1980s, the French government restored the tapestry and placed it in its own museum in Bayeux. It hangs in its own light-, temperature-, and humidity-controlled environment, where hopefully it will survive another one thousand years.

THE ORIGINAL LATIN

Panel 24   Hic Willelm dedit Haroldo arma

Panels 24–25   Hic Willelm venit Bagias

Panels 25–26   Ubi Harold sacramentum fecit Willelmo duci

Panels 26–27   Hic Harold dux reversus est ad Anglicam terram

Panel 28   et venit ad Edwardum regem

Panels 29–30   Hic portatur corpus Eadwardi regis ad ecclesiam
                      sancti Petri Apostoli

*This image shows Panels 29–30. Other images from the Bayeux
Tapestry can be seen on pages 56, 59, 61, 64, 73, 77, and 147.*

Panel 30   Hic Eadwardus rex in lecto alloquitur fideles

Panel 30   et hic defunctus est

Panel 31   Hic dederunt Haroldo coronam regis

Panel 31   Hic residet Harold rex Anglorum

A LITERAL TRANSLATION

Panel 24	Here William gave arms to Harold
Panels 24–25	Here William came to Bayeux
Panels 25–26	Where Harold made an oath to Duke William
Panels 26–27	Here Duke Harold returned to the English country
Panel 28	and came to King Edward
Panels 29–30	Here the body of King Edward is carried to the church of Saint Peter the Apostle
Panel 30	Here King Edward in bed talks to his faithful followers
Panel 30	and here he is dead
Panel 31	Here they have given the crown of the king to Harold
Panel 31	Here sits throned Harold, King of the English

TIMELINE

600s B.C.	Celtic people move to Great Britain from mainland Europe.
A.D. 43	The Romans invade Great Britain. Roman armies build roads and towns, including London.
EARLY 400s	The Romans leave Great Britain after almost four hundred years of occupation.
MID-400s	Angles, Saxons, and Jutes from northern Europe settle in Great Britain.
596	Augustine, an Italian monk, begins to convert the Anglo-Saxons to Christianity.
LATE 700s	Viking raiding parties begin to attack England.
EARLY 800s	Vikings attack northern France.
C. 890	King Alfred the Great begins to build burhs, or fortified towns, throughout England.
891	Compiling information from earlier documents, English monks begin to create *The Anglo-Saxon Chronicle*.
900s	English kings develop the fyrd, a civilian army.

911	Rolf the Viking takes control of the region later known as Normandy.
979	King Ethelred II takes the English throne.
991	Danish Vikings attack England. The Vikings defeat English forces at the Battle of Maldon.

Anglo-Saxon warriors of the tenth century get ready to defend their land in this nineteenth-century woodcut.

131

1002	King Ethelred II of England marries Emma, daughter of the duke of Normandy.
1016	Canute of Denmark becomes king of England. He divides southern England into four earldoms.

c. 1018	Godwin becomes the earl of Wessex.
1028	William, the son of Duke Robert I of Normandy, is born in the town of Falaise.
1034	Duke Robert embarks on a pilgrimage to Jerusalem.
1035	Duke Robert dies during his pilgrimage. Seven-year-old William becomes the duke of Normandy.
1042	Edward the Confessor becomes king of England. He begins construction on Westminster Abbey.
1045	King Edward marries Edith, daughter of Earl Godwin.
1047	With the assistance of Henry I, king of France, William defeats rebel forces at the Battle of Val-ès-Dunes.
1051 OR 1052	Duke William visits King Edward in England.
1053	Earl Godwin dies. His son Harold Godwinson becomes earl of Wessex.
1064	Harold Godwinson visits Normandy and makes an oath of fealty to William. Harold might also have promised to help William secure the English throne on this trip.

1065	The witan gathers near London for its regular Christmas meeting. Westminster Abbey opens.
1066	
JANUARY 4	On his deathbed, King Edward entrusts his kingdom to Harold Godwinson.
JANUARY 5	King Edward dies.
JANUARY 6	Harold Godwinson is crowned king of England at Westminster Abbey.

A nineteenth-century interpretation of Harold's coronation at Westminster Abbey

WINTER AND SPRING	William and Harold prepare for war. William sends representatives to the pope, asking the church to back his campaign against England.

APRIL	Halley's comet appears in the skies over England.
SUMMER	The English navy and fyrd guard the English Channel. Most troops are stationed at the Isle of Wight.
SEPTEMBER 8	English forces leave the Isle of Wight, believing an invasion will not come until spring.
MID-SEPTEMBER	Harold Hardraade, the king of Norway, lands his forces near York. King Harold marches north with his housecarls.
SEPTEMBER 20	Harold Hardraade defeats the northern earls at the Battle of Fulford.
SEPTEMBER 25	King Harold defeats the Norwegians at Stamford Bridge.
SEPTEMBER 27	The Norman fleet crosses the English Channel, arriving at Pevensey the next day.
SEPTEMBER 29	William occupies Hastings and begins to erect a fortification there.
OCTOBER 1	King Harold learns that the Normans have landed on the English coast. He begins marching his men south.
OCTOBER 13	King Harold and his soldiers arrive near Hastings.

OCTOBER 14	Norman troops defeat English forces at the Battle of Hastings. King Harold dies in battle.
MID-DECEMBER	William's troops arrive outside London.
DECEMBER 25	William the Conqueror's coronation takes place in Westminster Abbey.
1070	William's troops kill townspeople and destroy houses, farms, and churches in northern England, putting an end to serious rebellion against his rule.

In this nineteenth-century woodcut, Norman nobility and soldiers work to quash rebellion in the north.

1086	William orders a survey of the English kingdom. Known as the Domesday Book, the survey assesses the kingdom's resources, such as land, animals, and people.
1087	William the Conqueror dies in France. His middle son, William Rufus, succeeds him.
1154	Henry II comes to the throne in England. He is the first king of the Plantagenet dynasty.

GLOSSARY

BARON: a nobleman in continental Europe before the Norman Conquest. After the conquest, *baron* became a title of nobility in England too.

BURH: a fortified town in Anglo-Saxon England

CIVIL WAR: a war between opposing groups of citizens in the same country

CORONATION: the ceremony at which a new king or queen is crowned

DUKE: a regional ruler in mainland Europe. After the Norman Conquest, *duke* became a title of English nobility.

DYNASTY: a family of rulers that hands down power from one generation to the next

EARL: a regional ruler of Anglo-Saxon England

EXILE: to banish or expel someone from his or her home country

FEALTY: the loyalty and service a vassal must give to a lord

FYRD: the part-time militia, or citizen army, of Anglo-Saxon England

GELD: a tax in Anglo-Saxon and Norman England. *Geld* is an Old English word meaning "payment."

137

HOUSECARLS: the trained, professional soldiers of Anglo-Saxon kings

ILLUMINATED MANUSCRIPT: a handwritten book, adorned with illustrations. Illuminated manuscripts were common in the Middle Ages.

KNIGHT: a soldier who fought on horseback during the Middle Ages

LORD: a ruler to whom others owe service and obedience

MEDIEVAL: pertaining to the Middle Ages, the period between about A.D. 400 and 1400

MERCENARY: a soldier who fights for a foreign country in exchange for money

MONASTERY: a religious community for monks. Monasteries often include dormitories, churches, libraries, and farmland.

MONKS: men who have taken vows to lead lives devoted to God

NORMANS: people of the Normandy region of France. The Normans were descended from Viking conquerors. The place-name *Normandy* gets its name from the Vikings, or "north men."

PILGRIMAGE: a journey to a shrine or a sacred place made for religious purposes

POPE: the leader of the Catholic Church, with headquarters in Rome, Italy. At the time of the Norman Conquest, the Catholic Church was the sole Christian Church in Europe.

RELIC: an object, such as bones or other remains, associated with a saint. Relics are believed to carry the saint's spiritual power.

SERFS: farmers who received small pieces of land from a landowner in exchange for rent and additional work. Serfs in Anglo-Saxon England had few rights and were not free to leave the land they farmed.

SUCCESSION: the passing down of a throne, property, title, or other benefit from one person to another

THANE: a landowner in Anglo-Saxon England

VASSAL: a person under the protection of a lord, to whom he has vowed fealty

VIKINGS: Scandinavian pirates who raided territories in Europe from the late 700s to about 1100

WITAN: the council of advisers to the Anglo-Saxon king

MODERN ENGLISH WORD ORIGINS

Languages influence each other and evolve over time, incorporating new words, spellings, and pronunciations in the course of hundreds, if not thousands, of years. Many modern English words come from Old English, the language of Anglo-Saxon England. Many other modern English words come from Anglo-French, the version of French used in England after the Norman Conquest. On the following four pages are examples of modern English words and their cousins in the older languages from which they come.

WORDS FROM OLD ENGLISH

MODERN ENGLISH	OLD ENGLISH
bake	bacan
bath	baeth
bridge	brycg
brother	brothor
child	cild
cow	cu
craft	craeft
ditch	dic
dog	docga
drink	drincan
eat	aet

MODERN ENGLISH	OLD ENGLISH
field	feld
fight	feohtan
friend	freond
green	grene
house	hus
live	libban
love	lufu
merry	myrge
mother	modor
oats	ate
ox	oxa
plow	ploh
rain	regn
sheep	sceap
ship	scip
shirt	scyrte
shoe	scoh
sleep	slaep
stick	stician
stone	stan
watch	waeccan
wheat	hwaete
wood	widu
work	werc
wrong	wrang

WORDS FROM ANGLO-FRENCH (FRENCH SPOKEN IN MEDIEVAL ENGLAND)

MODERN ENGLISH	ANGLO-FRENCH
age	aage
aid	aider
attorney	aturné
beef	beof
button	butun
carry	carier
cattle	katil
cauldron	cauderon
change	changer
chimney	chiminee
court	curt
double	duble
duke	duc
felon	felun
govern	governer
journey	jurnee
jury	juree
justice	justise
language	langage
marriage	marier
mountain	muntaine
mutton	mutun

MODERN ENGLISH	ANGLO-FRENCH
nobility	nobilité
paint	peint
parliament	parlement
please	plaisir
quit	quiter
respond	respuns
royal	real
tailor	taillur
traitor	traitre

WHO'S WHO?

EDITH (1020–1075) Edith was the third child of Godwin,

the earl of Wessex, and sister to Harold Godwinson, Tostig, and their brothers. In 1045 her powerful father arranged her marriage to Edward the Confessor, probably to ensure that the Godwin family would inherit the English kingdom. However, the couple had no children. When Edward sent Edith's father and brothers into exile in 1051, he sent her to a nunnery. When her family members returned, she came back to court. About the time of Edward's death, Edith ordered a monk to write a biography of her husband. The book glorified the Godwin family and portrayed Edward as a saint. Edith died at Winchester.

EDWARD THE CONFESSOR (c. 1003–1066) Edward was

the son of Ethelred II and his second wife, Emma. After the Danes invaded England, when Edward was about ten, he went to live in Normandy. He came to the throne in 1042 but was not a strong leader. He was intensely religious and earned the name Edward the Confessor because he confessed, or spoke about, his religious faith. His greatest accomplishment was the construction of Westminster Abbey in London. He married Edith, daughter of Godwin, the powerful earl of Wessex, but they had no children. According to William the Conqueror, Edward promised him the English throne.

EMMA (985–1052) Born in Normandy, Emma was the

daughter of the Norman duke Richard I, but her destiny lay in England. She was married to two English kings, first to Ethelred II and then, after he died, to his enemy King Canute. Her children by Ethelred, including the future King Edward, grew up in Normandy. Hardecanute, her son by Canute, also ruled England briefly. William the Conqueror used his connection to his great-aunt Emma to legitimize his claim to the throne.

HAROLD GODWINSON (c. 1020–1066) Harold's father was Godwin, the earl of Wessex, a powerful man in the court of Edward the Confessor. After his father's death, Harold also became an earl and close adviser to the king. Harold was crowned King Harold II the day after Edward's death in January 1066. He was tall, patient, and cheerful. He did not mind criticism but was hard on those who broke the law. He demonstrated his abilities as a commander late in 1066 when he defended England against Harold Hardraade, king of Norway. A few weeks later, Norman invaders killed Harold during the Battle of Hastings.

HAROLD HARDRAADE (1015–1066) Harold Hardraade became king of Norway in 1047. He tried twice to invade Denmark but was unsuccessful both times. He finally made peace with Denmark in 1064. With his eye on the English throne, he invaded England in 1066 and was victorious at the Battle of Fulford. But Harold II's army killed him and most of his soldiers at Stamford Bridge. His name, Hardraade, meant "hard bargainer." Harold was brave, ruthless, and stubborn. He was very tall, with large hands and feet and a loud voice. He also wrote poetry.

HENRY I (1069–1135) Henry, William the Conqueror's youngest son, was born in England. His brother William Rufus took the English throne when their father died in France. When William Rufus died in 1100, Henry had himself crowned king of England. Henry married Matilda of Scotland, thereby establishing peace with England's northern neighbor. His nickname Henry Beauclerc ("fine scholar") indicates he was a well-educated man. He was an energetic and decisive king. He also earned the name Lion of Justice.

LANFRANC (c. 1005–1089) Born in Italy, Lanfranc was a

lawyer, teacher, and politician in Normandy. He joined a monastery at Bec, Normandy, where he lived a life of prayer and silence for several years. In 1063 Duke William made Lanfranc the first abbot of the new monastery at Caen. After the conquest, William asked Lanfranc to come to England. As archbishop of Canterbury from 1070 to 1089, Lanfranc oversaw important reforms to the English church. After William died, Lanfranc helped William Rufus take his father's place as king.

ODO (c. 1030–1097) After Herleve gave birth to William,  the future William the Conqueror, his father, Duke Robert, arranged for her to marry a Norman nobleman. They had two children, Odo and Robert. In 1049 Odo became bishop of Bayeux. He was with William at the Battle of Hastings. After the conquest, he became an extremely wealthy man, with vast landholdings in England. He often ruled the country in his brother's place while William saw to affairs in Normandy. Many historians believe Odo arranged for the creation of the Bayeux Tapestry, which shows his important role in the conquest.

WILLIAM I (c. 1028–1087) The son of Duke Robert I of Normandy and Herleve, a village woman, William succeeded his father as duke in 1035, at age seven. He spent much of his childhood and youth escaping from enemies and trying to hold on to his title. By the time he was an adult, he was an experienced military commander. He believed he was destined to succeed the childless Edward the Confessor as king of England. When that did not happen, he decided to invade the island kingdom. His troops won the Battle of Hastings in 1066, but it took

William several more years to suppress the English rebels who opposed his rule. As king, William did not spend a lot of time in England but instead spent many years dealing with political problems with Normandy's neighbors. He died in Rouen from an accidental injury and was buried in the abbey he had established at Caen.

SOURCE NOTES

4 Kevin Crossley-Holland, ed., *The Anglo-Saxon World: An Anthology* (Oxford: Oxford University Press, 1982), 257.

11 Allen R. Brown, *The Norman Conquest of England: Sources and Documents* (Woodbridge, Sussex: Boydell Press, 1984), 259.

14 Crossley-Holland, *The Anglo-Saxon World*, 246–49.

21 Ibid., 259.

23 Brown, *The Norman Conquest of England*, 150.

26 Ibid., 151.

28 Ibid., 94.

30 Crossley-Holland, *The Anglo-Saxon World*, 213.

31 Brown, *The Norman Conquest of England*, 94.

33 Crossley-Holland, *The Anglo-Saxon World*, 132.

35 Brown, *The Norman Conquest of England*, 149.

43 Ibid., 93.

44 Ibid., 9.

52 Ibid.

52 David C. Douglas, *William the Conqueror: The Norman Impact upon England* (Berkeley: University of California Press, 1992), 50.

58 Brown, *The Norman Conquest of England*, 93.

70 Ibid., 71.

72 Ibid., 69.

75 Ibid., 72–73.

75 Ibid., 71.

83 Ibid., 72.

84 Ibid.

91 Ibid., 78.

92 Ibid., 79.

98 Ibid., 105.

103 Ibid., 79.

110 Ibid., 116.

121 Henry of Huntingdon, *The History of the English People 1000–1154*, trans. Diana Greenway (Oxford: Oxford University Press, 2002), 6.

125 David M. Wilson, *The Bayeux Tapestry* (New York: Thames and Hudson, 1985), 172.

BIBLIOGRAPHY

PRIMARY SOURCES

The Anglo-Saxon Chronicle. In *The Anglo-Saxon World: An Anthology*. Edited by Kevin Crossley-Holland. Oxford, UK: Oxford University Press, 1982. *The Anglo-Saxon Chronicle* contains yearly descriptions of wars, the deeds of kings, and other historical events in Anglo-Saxon England. The chronicle covers events from the 400s to 1154. Entries from the 400s to 891 were compiled from earlier documents. After 892, various writers added brief reports of each year's events.

Beowulf. In *The Anglo-Saxon World: An Anthology*. Edited by Kevin Crossley-Holland. Oxford, UK: Oxford University Press, 1982. *Beowulf* is an epic, or extremely long, poem. It was written by an anonymous poet, probably in the eighth century. It is the story of a Swedish prince who helps the king of the Danes by killing two monsters. He returns home and is killed by another monster.

Henry of Huntingdon. *The History of the English People 1000–1154*. Translated by Diana Greenway. Oxford, UK: Oxford University Press, 2002. Henry begins his account with the marriage of King Ethelred II to Emma and ends with the death of King Stephen, an event that occurred in the author's lifetime.

Ordericus Vitalis. *The Ecclesiastical History*. In *The Norman Conquest of England: Sources and Documents*. Edited by Allen R. Brown. Woodbridge, Sussex: Boydell Press, 1984. Ordericus Vitalis was an English monk who lived from 1075 to 1142. He wrote *The Ecclesiastical History* in the early 1100s. The lengthy work examines the history of Christianity and the popes, the history of France and Normandy, the Norman Conquest, and the Norman kings of England.

William of Jumièges. *The Deeds of the Norman Dukes*. In *The Norman Conquest of England: Sources and Documents*. Edited by Allen R. Brown. Woodbridge, Sussex: Boydell Press, 1984. William of Jumièges, a Norman monk, was probably born around 1000. He wrote *The Deeds of the Norman Dukes* around 1070.

William of Malmesbury. *The Deeds of the Kings of the English*. In *The Norman Conquest of England. Sources and Documents*. Edited by Allen R. Brown. Woodbridge, Sussex: Boydell Press, 1984. Born in the late 1000s, William of Malmesbury takes his name from Malmesbury Abbey, where he lived as a monk. William wrote several books on English history. *The Deeds of the Kings of the English* covers the years 449 to 1127.

William of Poitiers. *The Deeds of William II, Duke of Normandy*. In *The Norman Conquest of England. Sources and Documents*. Edited by Allen R. Brown. Woodbridge, Sussex: Boydell Press, 1984. William of Poitiers worked for William the Conqueror and wrote his biography between 1071 and 1077. The early and concluding parts of the work have been lost. The existing text covers the years 1047 to 1068. The biography includes details on Norman preparations for the conquest, the Battle of Hastings, and events following the battle.

Wilson, David M. *The Bayeux Tapestry*. New York: Thames and Hudson, 1985. The Bayeux Tapestry is a series of pictures portraying the events of the Norman Conquest, from Harold's trip to Normandy to his death at the Battle of Hastings. The illustrations are accompanied by Latin descriptions. Wilson's book reproduces the images and text and provides scholarly commentary.

SECONDARY SOURCES

Campbell, James, Eric John, and Patrick Wormald. *The Anglo-Saxons*. London: Penguin Books, 1982. This book covers English history from the end of Roman Britain to the end of the Anglo-Saxon kings. It is beautifully illustrated and examines topics ranging from Anglo-Saxon coins to life in the burhs.

Chibnall, Marjorie. *Anglo-Norman England: 1066–1166*. Oxford, UK: Basil Blackwell, 1986. This book by a Cambridge University professor sheds new light on the way church reforms, population growth, increasing trade, and higher literacy levels helped shape Norman England.

The Domesday Book Online
http://www.domesdaybook.co.uk/index.html
This website describes how and why the Domesday Book was compiled. The site offers brief background articles on life in England in 1087, a timeline of William the Conqueror's life, and a glossary.

Douglas, David C. *William the Conqueror: The Norman Impact upon England*. Berkeley: University of California Press, 1992. This classic biography examines William's tumultuous youth, his conquest of England, and his rule over Norman England.

Fell, Christine. *Women in Anglo-Saxon England and the Impact of 1066*. London: British Museum Publications, 1984. This book uses myths, poetry, wills, charters, laws, and archaeological evidence to investigate the lives of women before, during, and after the eleventh century in England.

History of the Monarchy: Kings and Queens of England (to 1603)
http://www.royal.gov.uk/output/Page10.asp
This useful website has brief biographies of the kings and queens of England from 757 to 1603.

Howarth, David. *1066: The Year of the Conquest*. New York: Penguin Books, 1977. The author of this engaging tale speculates about what really happened in 1066 and the motives that drove William, Harold, and the other major players to behave the way they did.

McArthur, Tom, ed. *The Oxford Companion to the English Language*. New York: Oxford University Press, 1992. This reference book has articles on the Anglo-Saxons and Old English, as well as the Normans and Norman French.

The Norman Conquest
http://www.bbc.co.uk/history/war/normans/background_01.shtml
This website prepared by the British Broadcasting Corporation offers background material on the conquest and the individuals involved, as well as timelines, multimedia features, and links to related sites.

Reynolds, Susan. *Fiefs and Vassals*. Oxford, UK: Oxford University Press, 1994. In this scholarly book, Reynolds offers a new examination of social relations between lords and vassals in medieval society.

Stenton, Frank. *Anglo-Saxon England*. 3rd ed. Oxford: Oxford University Press, 1971. This book is the standard study of Anglo-Saxon England to which all historians refer. It covers the period from the withdrawal of the Romans to the death of William the Conqueror.

Tomkeieff, O. G. *Life in Norman England*. New York: Capricorn Books, 1966. Written for the general reader and illustrated with black-and-white photos and drawings, this book portrays life in England after the conquest.

Whitelock, Dorothy, David C. Douglas, Charles H. Lemmon, Frank Barlow, and C. T. Chevallier. *The Norman Conquest: Its Setting and Impact*. New York: Charles Scribner's Sons, 1966. This book of essays by leading experts was published to mark the nine hundredth anniversary of the Battle of Hastings. It provides an excellent introduction to the conquest period.

Williams, Ann. *The English and the Norman Conquest*. Woodbridge, Sussex: Boydell Press, 1995. The author, a historian, describes what happened to English people—from earls to abbots to servants—following the conquest.

FURTHER READING AND WEBSITES

BOOKS

Bennett, Matthew. *Campaigns of the Norman Conquest: Essential Histories.* Botley, UK: Osprey Publishing, 2001. This short book, written for a general audience, has lots of maps and drawings. It emphasizes the military aspect of the Norman Conquest.

Campbell, Kumari. *United Kingdom in Pictures.* Minneapolis: Twenty-First Century Books, 2004. This title from the Visual Geography Series takes a look at the people, land, history, culture, and economy of the United Kingdom.

Dyer, Christopher. *Making a Living in the Middle Ages: The People of Britain, 850–1520.* New Haven, CT: Yale University Press, 2002. In this social and economic study of medieval Britain, the author looks at land use, the growth of towns, and the role of trade over a seven-hundred-year period. The conquest period, 1050 to 1100, takes up one chapter.

Lacey, Robert, and Danny Danziger. *The Year 1000: What Life Was Like at the Turn of the First Millennium.* New York: Little Brown and Company, 1999. Published at the turn of the second millennium, this charming book bases each of its twelve chapters on a monthly illustration from the Julius Work Calendar.

Morris, Mark. *Domesday Revisited: A Traveler's Guide.* London: Severn House Publishers, 1987. The author visited some of the churches, castles, villages, and forests described in the Domesday Book. The text and photos describe how these places look in modern times and how they must have appeared a thousand years ago.

Stafford, Pauline. *Queen Emma and Queen Edith: Queenship and Women's Power in Eleventh-Century England.* Oxford, UK: Blackwell Publishers, 1997. This detailed biography examines the lives of the two early queens, as well as the role of women in Anglo-Saxon England.

WEBSITES

Conquest: Society of Anglo-Norman Living History
http://www.conquest.pwp.blueyonder.co.uk/
This site includes photographs from Battle of Hastings reenactments, as well as background on the equipment and warfare techniques of the period.

English Heritage
http://www.english-heritage.org.uk/server/show/nav.2 English Heritage is a group dedicated to preserving and promoting English history. It protects historic sites, such as Battle Abbey in Hastings. The group sponsors exhibits and educational activities, many of them dealing with the Norman Conquest. The website offers information on these programs and exhibits.

Medieval History Timeline Reference
http://www.TimeRef.com
This educational resource covers Britain from the years 1000 to 1500. It offers a timeline of events, maps, a translation of *The Anglo-Saxon Chronicle*, descriptions of important individuals, and family trees. Features on the architecture of the period include 3-D diagrams of castles and abbeys.

Monarchy: Battle of Hastings
http://www.channel4.com/history/microsites/M/monarchy/battles/hastings.html
This page is part of a history website put together by Britain's Channel 4 television. Designed for students, it includes a timeline of major events and brief articles on life and times throughout British history.

The Normans, A European People
http://www.norman-world.com/angleterre/index.htm
This website explores Normandy, Norman England, and the Normans in the Mediterranean region.

INDEX

157

ABOUT THE AUTHOR

Janice Hamilton is a writer and freelance journalist who worked for several years in the Montréal bureau of The Canadian Press. As a freelancer, she covers a wide range of issues, from the environment to immigration laws. Her articles have appeared in a variety of publications, including *Canadian Medical Association Journal* and *Canadian Geographic*. She is also the author of several recent Visual Geography Series titles. Ms. Hamilton lives in Montréal with her husband and two sons.

PHOTO ACKNOWLEDGMENTS

The images in this book are used with the permission of: © Snark/Art Resource, NY, pp. 5, 119; © Laura Westlund/Independent Picture Service, pp. 6, 71, 76; © Verena Worth/Alamy, p. 7; © The British Library, pp. 8, 10, 19, 24, 99, 120, 146; © North Wind Picture Archives, pp. 12, 33, 45, 53, 67, 74, 78, 79, 131, 135; The Art Archive/Bibliothèque Universitaire de Médecine, Montpellier/Dagli Orti, p. 13; © Gianni Dagli Orti/CORBIS, pp. 17, 73; The Art Archive/Bodleian Library Oxford, p. 22; © Hulton Archive/Getty Images, pp. 30, 35, 69, 80, 86, 144 (bottom); © HIP/Art Resource, NY, pp. 31, 32, 38, 41, 82, 89, 93, 145; © Erich Lessing/Art Resource, NY, pp. 34, 56, 122; © The British Library/Heritage-Images/The Image Works, p. 37; © Classic Image/Alamy, p. 42; The Art Archive/British Library, pp. 49, 96; © World History Archive/Alamy, p. 51; © Photononstop/SuperStock, p. 54; © Visual Arts Library (London)/Alamy, pp. 59, 128; © Bridgeman Art Library, London/SuperStock, p. 61; © Mary Evans Picture Library/The Image Works, pp. 63, 114, 133; © Archivo Iconografico, S.A./CORBIS, p. 64; © The British Library/HIP/The Image Works, p. 66; © INTERFOTO Pressebildagentur/Alamy, p. 77; © Archive Photos/Getty Images, p. 87; The Art Archive/Public Record Office London, p. 91; © Nancy Carter/North Wind Picture Archives, p. 101; © Steve Vidler/SuperStock, p. 105; © Vanni/Art Resource, NY, p. 107; © Scott Barbour/Getty Images, p. 111; © age fotostock/SuperStock, p. 112; Edith Finding the Body of Harold, 1828 (oil on canvas) by Vernet, Emile Jean Horace (1789–1863) © Musee d'Art Thomas Henry, Cherbourg, France/Giraudon/The Bridgeman Art Library Nationality/copyright status: French/out of copyright, p. 144 (top); The Art Archive/Musée de la Tapisserie Bayeux/Dagli Orti, p. 147.

Cover: © The Bridgeman Art Library/Getty Images.